OUR CHANGING SCOTLAND

A YEARBOOK OF SCOTTISH GOVERNMENT 1976-77

Edited by   M G Clarke   HM Drucker

EUSPB

To the much maligned governors of Scotland.

Printed and Bound only by T. & A. Constable Ltd.

Published by EUSPB 1 Buccleuch Place, Edinburgh

contents

Reference Section

contributors

1   C. H. Allen, BA is a Lecturer in Politics and a member of the Unit for the Study of Government in Scotland University of Edinburgh

2   M. G. Clarke, BA, MA, is an Honorary Fellow of the Politics Department, University of Edinburgh

3   H. M. Drucker, BA, PhD. is a Lecturer in Politics and Chairman of the Unit for the Study of Government in Scotland

4   John Firn, BA, NDA, SDA, is a Lecturer in Social and Economic Research, University of Glasgow

5   Brian Gill, MA, LLB, PhD is an Advocate

6   Drummond Hunter, MA, LLB, FHA is Secretary to the Scottish Health Service Planning Council

7   James G. Kellas is a Senior Lecturer in Politics, University of Glasgow

8   Elizabeth A. Masterman is an honours student of Politics; University of Edinburgh

9   Professor D. N. MacCormick, MA, is Professor of Public Law, University of Edinburgh

10   The Very Reverend Professor John McIntyre, MA, BD, DLitt, DD, is Professor of Divinity, University of Edinburgh

11   Professor D. I. MacKay is Professor of Political Economy, University of Aberdeen

12   Councillor W. J. McKechin is Vice Chairman of Strathclyde Education Committee

13   Colin McLean, MA, is Editor of the **Times Educational Supplement Scotland**

14 R. E. G. Peggie is Chief Executive of Lothian Regional Council

15 Father Anthony Ross is Chaplain to Heriot-Watt University and Chairman of the Parole Board

16 C. R. Smallwood MA, BPhil is Lecturer in Economics, University of Edinburgh

17 The Right Hon. Lord Wheatley is the Lord Justice Clerk

18 Archbishop Thomas Winning is Archbishop of Glasgow

We wish to record our thanks to the editors of **Question, The Scotsman** and **The Times Educational Supplement** (Scotland) for permission to reprint material which was originally published by them. We also wish to record out thanks to the trustees of the Moray Endowment, to Allan Drummond, Peter Stevenson, R. G. Duthie, D. G. MacDonald, James Jack, James Milne, Kathie Brown, St John Bates, Deyan Sudjic, G. H. Spiers, K. Duncan, J. Page, the political parties and the Scottish Information Office; and for their editorial help to Angela Clarke and Nancy Drucker.

Last but certainly not least - EUSPB Staff - Margaret Roxton, Moira Smith and Bill Spence.

M. G. CLARKE
H. M. DRUCKER

Our Changing Scotland

The Editors

Scotland is a perplexing place at present. It is on the threshold of a major constitutional reform which will greatly enhance its political life and which will change the course of its history in unpredictable ways. The debate about the nature of this reform must rate as one of the most important since the Union. A basic assumption of the debate seems to be that devolutionary settlement is inevitable - and certainly no political party is committed to anything else. Given this, it is difficult to generate excitement about what is being publicly contested - namely, institutional arrangements and relationships. And until the institutions are formed there is no real forum for the discussion of political issues in a Scottish context.

This is a shame. There are important questions to be asked and answered about the contents of the devolutionary package, and, in order to stimulate a sensible discussion, there is a place for a strong anti-devolutionary voice; there is also a need to look at the relationship of any new arrangements to existing institutions of government, without assuming that they will all be swept away. Parallel to both these discussions there should be some semblance of political debate about the needs of Scotland and the implications of today's economic and social problems.

Edinburgh University's Unit for the Study of Government in Scotland was created in the hope that it might act as a catalyst by bringing together people from inside and outside the world of government to discuss these issues. The publication of this **Yearbook** is an example of the enterprise. The intention is not that it should provide the answers to the pressing questions of the day but rather that it should serve as a focus for debate. Hence there are papers reviewing two major areas of governmental activity which have a distinctive Scottish mark and which have already undergone major reform; there are a series of papers on aspects of the current devolution debate, and there are discussions of some of the pressing political issues of the moment.

We have set outselves two tasks in this Introduction. We will underline some of the more important points made by our contributors, locate their papers in the current debate and relate them to one another. At the same time, we see it as our job in this **Yearbook** to emphasise some aspects and consequences of what is happening which are commonly overlooked. In this role we have tried to ensure some balance in the debate. This second task has forced us much against our own inclinations into a rather pessimistic view. For the fact is that political debate often proceeds by raising expectations. The debate about devolution is no exception, with all parties tempted to raise the expectations of their supporters. It is manifestly the responsibility of such a book as this to call attention to the more problematic consequences of what is proposed. We do this in no spirit of gloom, simply in the belief that dangers are less likely to be encountered if understood in advance.

It is intended that the **Yearbook** become an annual publication and, to this end, there is a bibliographical and reference section which will be brought up to date with each issue. There are a number of other subjects we had hoped to look at in this volume - recent developments in the working of the Scottish Office, the way in which Shetland has handled oil development, the early experience and prospects of the Scottish Development Agency, and the effects of the cuts in public|expenditure on the personal social services, to name but four. Plans are in hand for the 1977 volume, which will pursue these and other matters. By the time of its publication the first District Council elections and perhaps a General Election will have taken place. There will also be considered comment on these.

II

Few people, it seems, appreciate in anything more than a general way the problems which government at national level face and the difficulties which politicians and administrators have in resolving them. It is hoped that the essays which follow will help in sowing some of the seeds of understanding. There can be few things more misunderstood than the re-organisation of local government or apparently faceless than the Scottish Office. Robert Peggie's paper encompasses the former but it has proved difficult to get an informed account of the latter's operation. This raises a problem which must be overcome. There is too great a reluctance - stemming from the legal inhibitions of the Official Secrets Acts and the informal conventions which surround them - for insiders in central government to write about what they see around them. Of course, no practising politician or official can be expected to write in a detailed way about either his day-to-day existence or his colleagues, but there is a happy medium between this and a description of the organisation chart.

This same reluctance to describe how the machnine of central government works seems also to inhibit conversation with informed outsiders so that second hand pictures can be painted. Yet interested citizens will begin to understand how daily business is conducted and the kinds of problems which confront their governors only when the shrouds are lifted.

A rational reformer of Scottish government, able to ignore the external world and the passage of time, would not have considered a reform of local government or the health service or, possibly, the creation of a Scottish Development Agency - let alone membership of the European Economic Community - as separable from the design of the devolution package. Had the Conservative government of 1970 been able to forsee, in 1971 or 1972, that nationalism had not 'gone away', a devolutionary settlement primarily with an administrative base and linked with local government reform might have produced a system of government entirely different from the one we are now envisaging - and incidentally had a considerable impact on the course of party politics. But then politics is not an entirely rational business and the steady march of events cannot be ignored. Rightly or wrongly, particular problems usually have to be viewed in their own temporal context, and such are the pressures, sorted out on their own merits.

One such problem was the reform of the Health Service, which is discussed in Drummond Hunter's paper. The reform was conceived and executed as the result of changes within the Health Service itself. The new system, Hunter suggests, is flexible enough, and tied closely enough to the control of those who have to operate it, to be able to adjust to new situations as they arise. In the immediate future, instead of thinking of hospitals and doctors as machines and technicians producing healthy people who can return to the community - rather like so many serviced cars returning to the road from a few expensive garages - we shall have to start thinking about the creation of a 'healthy community'. What we need is not so much a health service as a health policy. Scots have fewer teeth per head than the citizens of any other industrialis nation. Bad dentistry? No - bad diets. What does devolution have to do with all this? Very little; but Hunter, like others. is uneasy about the prospect of 'political' interference in a situation which is complicated enough as it is.

The work of contemporary democratic government is both complex and difficult. Most of the essays in this volume refer implicity to this problem. The prospect of a devolution of executive and legislative power to an elected assembly raises some of these complexities though it is far from certain that it will resolve them. We have to keep several conflicting necessities in mind. Our government should be accountable to those whom it governs. This is the strongest constitutional (as opposed to 'Scottish') argument for devolution: we need a public check on the activities of the Scottish Office. But while being accountable, our government must also have reasonably clear and tolerably consistent political direction. Such direction must not change too frequently. Accountability without clear, consistent and constant policy can simply be a recipe for **ad hoc** populism. It is also very inefficient. The consequences of policy changes often take years to be felt. If we change policies too frequently no one benefits and our social problems simply fester while representative government loses credibility with the electorate. In addition, we need to attract competent trained professional advisers into public affairs and once we have them, to ensure that their expertise is used. Our social problems will not yield to amateurs. We live in a technologically sophisticated society and we need the advice of those trained to handle our complicated machinery if we're to master it. We also need skilled administrators to hold the loose ends of policy together and, finally, we need an informed public opinion.

The administrative reforms which have taken place in advance of devolution have been intended to achieve some or all of these objectives. As the paper on local government shows, reorganisation was based on the considerations of the Wheatley Report though a number of changes were made both inside and outside Parliament to meet particular interests. It is unfortunate that structural reorganisation did not go hand-in-hand with a revision of the financial base and that the pressures of inflation have made the new authorities unpopular before they have had a chance to prove themselves. The Layfield Committee's report has opened up the debate about the financing of local authorities, and thus, once again, the debate about the relationship between central and local government. The prospects are heartening for local government in England and Wales. For Scotland the question is complicated by the prospective relationships of local authorities to the Assembly.

Many observers and most ratepayers underestimated the time it would take for the trauma of reorganisation to be left behind and for the system to settle down (an important pointer to the difficulties the Assembly and its administration will have?). The issue is now whether the system will ever settle. If the Assembly and its Executive decide that they want to be seen to be responsible for the good government of Scotland, as well as for the passage of devolved legislation, then there will inevitably be conflict between them and the local authorities and pressure for another reform. The knowledge of this is disturbing to councillors and officials who are already reeling under public attack for many things outside their control and who are, at the same time, having to cope with severe curtailment of expenditure in areas of provision in which the public has become accustomed to growth.

Local government must go on to the offensive if it is to secure satisfactory working relationships with the Assembly. There is every reason for it to do so. An Assembly sitting in Edinburgh is no substitute for **local** government and the arguments which have traditionally supported the idea of democratically elected local institutions with their own administrative system are as pertinent now as they ever were. What is important is that a **modus operandi** be established.

As Peggie argues, it is probably too early to assess adequately the successes and failures of reorganisation. There are certainly widespread reservations about the two tier system and, with the Assembly, Scots will have substantial grounds for complaining of over-government. There is near universal agreement that it was mistaken to detach housing from regional provision of education and social work. And history may judge the reorganisation badly because while the interdependence of local authority activities has been accepted in principle, the traditional committee structure has been left pretty well intact. Further, nothing has been done to create a general administrative cadre who could in time spread across all departments and, like their counterparts in the civil service, develop networks within which business could be done.

III

It is worth noting that whereas the importance of the politician's role the need for clear political direction has been recognised in local government, the reformed Scottish Health Service has appeared to turn a blind eye to these issues. The health service is not directly responsible to any elected body and the influence of its professionals and managers has been increased. The Health Boards are composed of individuals nominated or appointed with no recognisable constituency and consequently uncertain in their role. The medical profession has argued before and since its nationalisation that it should be distanced from politicians. The two organisational charts of the health service in Scotland discussed by Hunter give the game away. The older structure is shown in a chart which clearly indicates that final authority goes through the Secretary of State to Parliament. The chart of the recently reorganised service stops with the Secretary of State. No mention of Parliament is made. A neater illustration of the administrators' and the professionals' recurrent day dream is hard to imagine. But there is a serious question here. Surely the allocation of medical resources involves political choice as much as the allocation of, say, educational resources? If this is so, then as financial resources become scarcer so the importance of public involvement in the debate about priorities will increase. As Drummond Hunter points out, modern medicine is so expensive that its control is inevitably a political issue.

Fear of political interference is also a factor in the argument about whether the universities should be devolved. Yet Professor John McIntyre is surely right to argue that the future proximity of government to the universities need not work to their detriment. In 1976-77 the University Grants Committee is giving one-eighth of its building allocation to the London School of Economics, so that the School, which is not a mile from Westminster, can convert a warehouse into a new library. Baleful influence? For many reasons nonetheless, there are are people in Scotland who fear that the universities may be treated less favourably than other institutions of higher education by a Scottish Assembly. More to the point, they may be treated less favourably than they are now. One feature of the universities which McIntyre discusses is that they, like Janus, face in two directions - to the Scottish school system and to the international world of scholarship and science. Many university teachers feel that a Scottish Assembly may fail to understand or respect their participation in this

9

world.

Political control of the judicial system raises no fewer thorny issues. Indeed, because the judicial system is of such fundamental importance to the liberty of people in our society, the issues are even more complex. We print two articles on this subject.

Lord Wheatley is the Lord Justice Clerk. When he rose in the House of Lords in January he gave the considered view of the High Court judges on the role they might play in a devolved scheme. This incidentally, was a question which the White Paper had left unresolved. But his speech is not just a response to the White Paper. His discussion of the issues of accountability, of professional standards and of jucicial independence is resonant beyond our immediate situation. Above all, he is concerned to protect the independence and integrity of the courts. These, he fears, might be endangered by a proximate Assembly. There would be a danger of political control.

Professor MacCormick joins the debate at just this point. The truth is, he says, that the values Lord Wheatley wishes to defend are supremely political. The desire to preserve - or create - an independent, non-partisan judiciary is at the heart of our system of political values. The question between them is this: Whom do you trust? Those who are against devolution do not trust a Scottish Assembly - but they may have to live with it.

IV

Whatever the shape of the devolutionary settlement, its financial and economic context becomes increasingly clear. The entire public sector is facing increasingly uncomfortable decisions as the full import of the government's determination to hold down real levels of public expenditure is driven home. Whether or not the beleagured White Paper on Public Expenditure takes too optimistic a view of the next few years is immaterial: its projections are in any case bleak. The health service and local government are not alone in having to reappraise the services they offer and the number of staff they employ. All sectors of government are officially or unofficially reviewing even the most draconian of alternatives open to them. This is easier in some areas than others. There is no doubt that for social work, for example, the agonies are extreme. Local authority social work departments have grown rapidly over the years since the generic service was created, so inculcating an expectation of continuing expansion. This is bad enough, but it has been made worse by an ever increasing volume of legislation and central government directives imposing obligations which require more resources if they are to be met.

All this does not augur well for an Assembly. It is likely to arrive on the scene unable to flex its muscles very much, caught in the financial squeeze of the moment. Few would deny that there is fat to be lost in the public sector or that a review of public provision is a good thing: it is just that it is easier to talk about than to do. For politicians it is especially difficult for they live by their aspirations and these are usually met by expansion.

There are few votes to be won by cutting services and there is no glamour attached to 'discussing priorities' when what that means is that the items at the bottom of the list will be lost without trace. To ask politicians to do this at the moment when they are trying to establish new political institutions and to be seen to govern better than their distant predecessors is to cry for the moon. Nevertheless, it is the real world that has to be managed and whether politics is the art of the possible or the impossible, the problems remain the same.

John Firn demonstrates the demands - and the difficulties - for economic policy. It is of no comfort to the present Secretary of State that he presides over the worst problems or urban deprivation in Western Europe and it will be no comfort to an Assembly either. The dilemmas posed by the industrial degeneration of the West are acute and it is manifestly unrealistic to believe that the spin-off of oil will be the panacea. It is salutary to be reminded, for example, that the electronics industry which appeared to be the saviour of Fife a decade ago has been caught badly short in the recession. It is also politically and socially naive to argue, as one recent commentator has done, that the West should be allowed to die and that new development should be concentrated in the East. Scotland's economic difficulties are deep-rooted and require bold new thinking. MacKay and Smallwood demonstrate that there is no unanimity among economists!

Would an independent Scotland be more prosperous than a devolved Scotland? As the two essays we present on this subject show, one's answer to this question depends on the answers given to a number of other questions. What, first, of all, is 'independence'? Any potential economic advantage of independence would depend on the terms agreed by the separating parties over such matters as North Sea Oil and the national debt. It is impossible to believe that English politicians could get parliamentary approval for a settlement which gave Scotland complete control over all the hydrocarbons in the North Sea. But now much would be given?

Another question arises over the political ability of the leaders of a newly independent Scotland to postpone the economic benefits of independence while the oil money was invested in new productive plant. The temptation would be to have 'jam today' - to spend any 'oil money' on immediate consumption. Indisputably, Scotland has its share of poverty - problems which increased supplementary benefits and pensions, decreased council house rents and rates could do a lot to alleviate in the short run. But if 'oil money' is to be of lasting benefit to future generations short run measures must be avoided. Increased consumption would add little to Scotland's productive capacity. In the first instance it would largely be a boon to foreign manufacturers. Again the judgement is political. MacKay believes we can trust a Scottish government to invest its revenues wisely: Smallwood is sceptical.

It is important in this respect to note that there are a number of challenges to the basic assumptions of the devolution debate from the industrial world. While it can readily be agreed that, in some sense, Scotland is most likely to solve well Scotland's problems, the argument can

11

easily become polemic. There are those who think that the uncertainty of the upheaval, the unpredictability of a new group of politicians and the possibilities of the 'slippery slope' becoming a reality, will be enough to frighten off those with a lot to lose. Capitalists and entrepreneurs are one obvious group. While experience can only confirm or deny the argument, it is one of which we should not lose sight.

V

Our political environment is changing in many ways. Devolution is but one of them. Some of the other changes have nothing to do with devolution but will pose problems for the devolved Assembly as soon as it is established. Religious education is one such issue - and a politically explosive one at that. Within the past year there has been an interesting debate amongst Roman Catholics about the continued existence of a separate Roman Catholic, though state supported, school system. There is good reason for wider public interest in this debate. Separate religious school systems are supported by public money and established by law. Secondly, separate systems provide separate career ladders for teachers so that churches retain a certain amount of patronage - no small advantage for minority groups. Thirdly, there is a political issue. The Roman Catholic population in Scotland, which is approximately one-sixth of the whole, is concentrated in and around Glasgow. This same area is the Labour Party's traditional stronghold. According to a poll of voters in that area taken shortly after the February 1974 election, no fewer than 79.3 per cent of Catholics who had voted had voted Labour. The community of interest between Church leaders and Labour politicians hardly needs underlining.

Archbishop Winning started the present round of the debate in his pastoral letter in February of this year. In the letter, which we reprint, he attacks the increasingly secular nature of education. This, he believes, will undermine support for Catholic education amongst Catholic parents. From the debate which has followed, some of the contributions to which we print, it is clear that not all Catholics think that the present system is the best way to preserve The Faith. It is also clear that educational and religious arguments have been mixed with those of self-interest and party political advantage. For example, as Colin McLean notes, the Labour Party cannot make up its mind. This is not surprising since the party is torn between an ideological commitment to comprehensive education and a practical need not to shake the very bedrock of its electoral support.

One valuable feature of the present system of Westminster based politics is that, so far as Scotland is concerned, it has served to obscure sectarian politics. Under the now defunct two-party system, both parties were content not to dwell on their sectarian support. It suited both for the Catholic minority to be enveloped in the Labour vote. In this situation the clergy, and especially the Catholic clergy, had considerable indirect power. Democrats are forced to condemn such indirect power on principle. But can anyone be sure that the break-up of the old system will not lead to the formation of purely sectarian groupings? Is there anyone who would welcome that prospect?

12

VI

The nature of the political debate in general and the devolution debate in particular raises the question of scale. There are no rules about what size of community can support political institutions, but there are fair questions to be asked about the space needed for political life to flourish. The running has been made in recent years by the advocates of small units. Empire is to be replaced by Community. The trend is international: participation in place of representation, anonymous bureaucracies are old hat; decisions are to be made by those whom they affect; uniform standards are unnecessary. Nationalist movements are breaking up nation states in much of the world: Canada, Lebanon, Northern Ireland, France, Spain, Ethiopia, Pakistan, Nigeria, and now Scotland and Wales.

Several different arguments are brought to bear by the advocates of smaller units of government. Each has been invoked on behalf of and adapted to Scotland. The first argument is for self-rule by 'natural communities'. Scotland is taken to be a natural community of Scots and Britain an unnatural agglomeration of peoples. The second argument is for rule by those who know from personal experience the conditions over which they rule. This is an argument for governing units which include small numbers of people. Devolution of purely Scottish concerns accords with this argument. Both of these are arguments of principle. They are supported by arguments from history. It is urged that the nation-state was a necessity in the early period of vigorous capitalism, but is less relevant in an age of international capitalism and of international organisations.

All these arguments ignore, where they do not indirectly controvert, some of the more painful lessons of eighteenth and nineteenth century political and social history. It may, for example, be more difficult to sustain a notion of 'private space' in the less tolerant, less diverse world of 'natural communities'. Religious tolerance, to mention one problem, which had become somewhat less troublesome in the large, diverse, anonymous nation-state, could become a worry again. To be blunt about it, public opinion is not always constant or wise. It is at least arguable that a smaller political world will lend itself more easily to manipulation by passionate rhetoric. In such a world it might be difficult for minorities to find a niche. Devolution fightens the privileged, for the privileged are, by definition, minorities. But devolution also worries the aptly named Scottish Minorities Group - a pressure group for the rights of homosexuals - and their distinction is no privilege. The debate about our changing government must consider who may lose as well as who may gain.

The distinction between proximate and distant control is perhaps one of degree. In the relatively restricted space of Scotland, with its relatively small population,the politicians (those political actors, that is, who act in public) will quite simply know more about what is going on. We may expect, in the first instance, that whatever devices the Assembly invents to correspond with Parliamentary Questions will elicit more useful and pertinent information than the present Westminster practices. This surely will be a gain.

One of the most resonant of the arguments in favour of small states derives from Rousseau. The argument is that only in small states can all men participate in governing and only by governing can men develop their full potential for responsible action. It is frequently suggested that devolution or independence will make Scots more responsible, more energetic and more enterprising. This too is an attractive argument. Certainly if it were true then devolution or independence would create a richer Scotland. Yet it is worth remembering that one of the arguments against the old local government system was that it required too many councillors to run it. The reformers hoped that the new system, which has room for approximately one-half of the number of councillors would encourage new men to come and and force the weakest of the old out. It is too early to judge the new system in this respect. It is, in any case, absurd to expect many intelligent and energetic people to give up paid employment, or accept lower remuneration in paid employment in order to spend half of their time being unpaid councillors.

It is conceivable, of course, that the advent of the Assembly will attract a young generation of public spirited people who would not otherwise have entered public life. But this new crop will take time to ripen and who will run the Assembly meantime?

VII

As James Kellas shows, it is unlikely that political activity after devolution will be a simple continuation of the present pattern. Nor are we likely to return to two-party politics for the foreseeable future. If we cannot go as far as to believe that 'Right' and 'Left' will soon as as irrelevant as 'Cavalier' and 'Roundhead', it is certainly plausible to suggest that the importance formerly accorded that distinction will diminish. It is interesting, in this light, that 'Right' and 'Left' in no way correspond to 'anti' or 'pro' devolutionist or 'pro' or 'anti' unionist. At the moment we have a multi-party system. As things stand and assuming the present electoral system, each of the main parties would have some seats at Westminster, some in the Assembly and some in local government.

As Kellas has reminded us more than once, Scotland has not had a two-party system since the Second World War. Since 1967 there have been four main parties and there is now a fifth in the reckoning. Two important points should be made about this. Firstly, there is no reason to believe that there is anything magical about two, three, four or five. Indeed, once there are more than two the incentive for keeping the parties intact is decreased. Our three largest parties - Conservative, Labour and National - are all coalitions; any of them could divide. Evidence from elsewhere suggests that proportional representation, currently a fasionable idea, could assist such fissiparous tendencies. Some might initially welcome such developments on the grounds that they would allow more straightforward representation of the views of different groups of citizens. However, beside the apparent advantages have to be set the disadvantages of small groups locked in conflict round relatively small sets of issues. Coalitions within parties are advantageous when it comes to the resolution of conflict and the business of the daily compromise of political life.

Our second point is this: a party rarely springs into existence and grows to maturity unless it represents an important group in society. Each of the parties is therefore likely to need the support of an identifiable group of voters. Differences between parties will give expression to the differences between these groups: this expression may accentuate the original social divisions.

There are a number of social divisions within Scotland, any one of which could prove important. The most obvious is between the West Central industrial area - roughly Strathclyde Region - and the rest. Already the argument about how to spend the oil revenues is partly an argument between Strathclyde (favouring consumption) versus the East (favouring industrial investment). Strathclyde has an identifiable community of interest and a history of insularity which, since it contains about half the electorate, may lead its representatives to organise against a coalition of everyone else.

Another obvious division is between Scotland's rural and urban areas. Scotland has two different and equally intractable social problems - the decay of central Strathclyde and the Highlands. The highlanders might easily feel called upon to unite in defence of their interests against those of the industrial areas. Both Conservatives and National parties would have much to lose if such a division emerged. The highland voters might want a party they could trust, not one dominated by the central industrial belt; least of all one dominated by Strathclyde. Geographically based divisions are not the only possibilities. As we mentioned before, sectarian differences might achieve political expression.

As Kellas shows, a number of English anti-devolutionists have opposed devolution because they fear it as the first step to separation. They see the Assembly as a platform for separatist demands, and this is also the Nationalist view. In that case our changing Scotland is in for a shock. We think these prognostications overdone. There is a danger, to be sure, that the presently envisaged changes will become uncontrollable. But it is also possible that once an Assembly is set up it will domesticate the wilder men. Power moderates. Indeed, it strikes us that now that an Assembly has been promised by all parties, the real threat to orderly progress arises from frustration. If this government in unwilling or unable to deliver a bill and pass it into law, the expectations it has raised could create a cynical, perhaps even a violent reaction.

The government lacks a majority - yet it has raised high hopes of major constitutional changes in Scotland. What happens if it falters or calls a General Election before an Act is passed? Will a triumphant Conservative government have more pressing things on its mind? Will the present leadership of the National Party be swept away in an impatient populist drive for independence? What would happen if a new extremist National Party leadership treated unsuccessfully for independence? There are many possibilities: the **status quo** is not one of them.

Whatever happens, we are manifestly living in a changing, even a rapidly changing, and certainly a fascinating Scotland. If we have taken it upon ourselves in this Introduction to point to some of the usually overlooked or underestimated dangers hidden within that change, that is not because we are gloomy. Far from it. Partly because of the political changes going on within it, Scotland is alive and exciting. Its government is much more interesting than it was until very recently, and, to us at least, it makes the rest of Great Britain seem dull.

Local Government reorganisation

R.G.E. Peggie

The question is often posed in discussion about local government reorganisation - "Was it necessary? Would it not have been in the public interest to restructure the existing authorities rather than go through the monumental task of introducing an entirely new system?"

The question is a fair one and, for those who have been through the trauma of reorganisation, the temptation is there to introduce a note of scepticism. However, to obtain an answer to the question it is necessary to examine the importance of local democracy in the governmental system of the country. It is interesting to note that the remit given to Lord Wheatley and his Royal Commission on Local Government stated "the need to sustain a viable system of local democracy" - which he defined "as that form of government in which the supreme power is vested in the people collectively and is administered by them or by representatives apppointed by them".

What constitutes a viable system of local democracy is of course a matter of judgement and experienced observers for long enough had identified that local government was a less effective force in the community, no longer held in high esteem and somehow ill-equipped to discharge its responsibilities. It is almost impossible to be certain of the initial reasons underlying this loss of confidence; what is certain, however, is that central and local government alike contributed in large measure to the situation which compelled the Royal Commission to open its report with the words: "Something is seriously wrong with local government in Scotland".

Since the end of the Second World War, central government had adopted a centralist approach to the provision of major public services and progressively new sections of the service had been created out of former local government responsibilities. Trunk Roads 1946; the hospital service 1947; Electricity 1947; Gas 1948; Water 1949; Harbours 1964. In its defence, central government will no doubt point to the additional responsibilities placed upon local authorities, the most significant being social work in 1968. It seems clear, however, that but for reorganisation this trend would have continued with passenger transport executives extended to the main centres of population and active consideration given to the creation of national police and education boards.

During this period when fundamental changes were affecting its role, local government for a variety of reasons now well recorded by Maud, Mallaby and Wheatley, continued to demonstate its inability to argue the case for local democracy or to display the qualities of leadership and management to ensure its continued existence as an important part of the democratic system in the country. It is contended that far from being an unnecessary and wasteful exercise reorganisation was timely in preserving the opportunity for local people to remain involved in the issues which vitally affect their lives. The form that the scheme of reorganisation took will, of course, be subject to debate and discussion for some considerable time to come. Clearly, something had to be done and Lord Wheatley's solution was one way of doing it.

Parliament brought about a number of major changes to the Royal Commission's recommendations, none more so than the transfer of responsibility for housing from regional authorities to district authorities. Lord Wheatley had argued that it was essential to place housing in the same authority as education and social work, thus bringing the sensitive personal services together under one unified control. In the event, the parliamentarians concluded that without housing the district authorities would have too little responsibility having only local amenity services to control. The consequent danger being that public spirited people would not be disposed to serving on authorities with powers so limited. Parliament may have been right in its assessment of the willingness of people to serve but their action is at the root of much of the difficulty in the relationship between the two levels of authority. In time that single transfer of function may provide the most convincing argument against the two-level system of local government. It would be unfortunate if Lord Wheatley was left to carry the responsibility for failure.

Following the publication in 1971 of the White Paper on the Future of Local Government in Scotland an initiative was taken by the existing local authority associations to commission a study of the organisational problems and to provide guidance on organisation and management structures for consideration by the new authorities. This initiative led to the formation of the Paterson Committee and their report had a powerful impact on the new authorities which assumed executive control in May of 1975. The designers of the new system had a number of significant factors to take into account in advancing their recommendations.

18

First, the size of the new authorities. The largest authority under the old system was Glasgow Corporation. That authority was to be absorbed in part in the giant Strathclyde Region taking responsibility for half the population of Scotland and throughout the country the pattern was the same: size adding a new dimension to the problem of management and control.

Second, the transfer from central government to local government of the responsibility for the preparation of regional strategic plans, that is, responsibility for economic, social and physical plans for the regions. This transfer represented a considerable devolution of power to the new authorities and presented them with new political possibilities. In this, local government had for the first time an opportunity to play a part in identifying the needs of local people and articulating those needs in a logical and persuasive way to central government in the hope of influencing national policies.

Third, it was envisaged that the opportunities afforded to exert political influence would induce the national political parties to participate in local government to a greater extent than ever before. By tradition, the Labour Party had been active in local politics operating under the national party banner and were much in evidence throughout the central belt of Scotland. On the other hand, the Conservative Party had not actively pursued a place in local politics and indeed the national organisation deliberately avoided involvement. It would be interesting to know the effect, if any, this lack of involvement had in conditioning the attitude of the Government members during the committee stages of the Local Government Bill. In the event, the forecast of political involvement was remarkably accurate. The Conservative Party restructured the local party machine and fought the election in 1974 under the national party banner. The Scottish National and Liberal Parties' efforts at that time were sporadic not through lack of interest in local government but through a calculated judgement not to overstretch national resources at a critical time.

Fourth, the expressed view that local government administration had not kept pace with new developments in management and that by tradition the structure of local government was excessively departmentalised. There was an identified lack of co-ordination and control and inadequate efforts were being made to reconcile plans with the resources likely to be placed at the disposal of the elected members.

Quite obviously these factors had a profound effect on the recommendations made by the Paterson Committee to the new authorities. At Member level the recognition of a heightening of political activity conditioned the introduction of a Policy and Resources Committee at the centre of the member organisation designed to facilitate the formulation of policy and to effect the difficult task of reconciling the needs of the community with the resources available. The marshalling of needs into priority ranking had for long enough exposed the weakness of the traditional structure.

The principle of such a committee was readily accepted by all political parties and most individual members but the composition of the committee stimulated a deal of controversy. The Paterson Committee recommended that the Policy and Resources Committee should consist solely of majority party members with suitable provision for keeping minority parties adequately informed. There is a strongly expressed contrary view which suggests thatwithoutthe influencing voice of members of minority parties the single party policy committee is in danger of pursuing wholly partisan policies without regard to minority interests or minority views. The advocates of the single party system are clearly in the minority in Scotland as only Strathclyde and Lothian have adopted that approach, the other Regions having opted for a multi-party system. It is much too early to make an assessment of the relevance of these arguments but no doubt time will expose evidence for and against both systems.

The other committee arrangements follow more traditional and conventional lines with members organised on an all-party básis into functional committees representing the main functions of the authority. The administrative arrangements are geared to co-ordinate and control the provision of services to the public and are designed to assist members in the formulation of policy. It is not surprising therefore to find universal acceptance of a structure having at its centre the means to draw the many strands of service provision together. The concept as envisaged by Paterson of a cohesive team with an acknowledged leader working to a common set of objectives has been implemented in both regional and district authorities.

The significance of the changes introduced on reorganisation has been obscured by the national economic climate and the unprecedented rates burden placed upon ratepayers coincident with the emergence of the new authorities. In the twelve months since reorganisation judgements have been distorted by a financial climate only partly of the new authorities' own making and very little account has been taken of the logistical problems encountered in creating some 65 new out of the 430 old authorities. Certainly, much of the criticism is unfair and ill founded, but the fact remains that the new authorities are operating in a climate which suggests that something is still wrong with local government. It is obvious that time is not on the side of members and officials to restore public confidence in local democracy. Perhaps it is not so much change but the speed of change which has created the crisis.

There is much in the achievements of the past twelve months to encourage the advocates of change and to provide political scientists with a rewarding area of research into evolving political influences. The new planning system designed to change the emphasis from land use planning to a more comprehensive form of planning taking greater account of the political realities and the constraints on resources, although as yet only at the formative stage, has clearly indidcated the potential for political influence. Until that potential is realised the influence exerted on national government by local government will be confined to initiatives taken by individual local councillors.

There is little evidence to suggest that government Ministers are any more willing now than they were in the past to take account of local initiatives. The regional reports required under the new system of planning are seen to be the proper vehicles for the projection of regional political policies. It will be interesting to observe how regional authorities propose to deal with the main issues identified in their first reports. It is suggested that those Councils with clearly identified political objectives will tend to apply stronger pressure on central government than those not so organised. The example of Strathclyde and the major issue of Stonehouse New Town provides a clue to future influences arising out of a regional report.

Success in this field will depend largely on how quickly local government politicians respond to their new-found opportunities. It has been difficult for experienced councillors to adjust to new concepts of policy making and control and many have continued to be overly involved in the day to day management of the authority. This temptation to look inwards rather than outwards, especially by members of policy committees, will restrict the capacity of the new authorities to create a significant influencing role. There is more than a lingering doubt in the minds of many councillors that withdrawal from day to day management means giving up power to the officials. There are some encouraging moves in the right direction but there is little doubt that the majority have a long way to go before accepting completly Lord Wheatley's view that a councillor's responsibility is to make sure that the machine works, not to work it himself.

Although the Council is the supreme policy making body, the affairs of the authority are in the main conducted through the committee system and the introduction of a policy committee into an otherwise traditional structure of functional committees has posed many problems for councillors and officials. Those who are members of a policy committee are given responsibility for the formulation of policy and many would see themselves as members of a Cabinet; a group of natural leaders enjoying the confidence of their colleagues. In practice, the existence of functional committees and the fact that in most cases the policy committee is composed of chairmen of those committees tends to leave members of the policy committee less certain of themselves in major issues affecting their service. This can lead the member to assume a more defensive role than would otherwise be desirable in looking at the wider aspects of policy matters. Again the existence of a strong party group can curtail the activities of the natural leaders, thus discouraging them from moving rapdily forward in an innovative sense. Conversely, membership of a functional committee can be frustrating for the backbench member. Opportunities to contribute to the formulation of policy are limited and decisions on major issues appear to be made before the views of minority interests are properly considered. This series of complex relationships can result in suspicision and disharmony among members and between groups and can put at risk the difficult relationship between councillor and official.

There is no real parallel between the operation of local councils and the operation of parliament and to regard regional councils as mini-parlaiments is hardly appropriate. Rather than attempt to create the image of parliament in local government, councillors must focus attention on what the public and the media now regard as failures of representation and accountability and find solutions that organisationally place the elected member in a position to better represent the interests of his electoral area and at the same time honour his commitments to the wider community.

Prior to reorganisation much was written about corporate management and many councillors and officials waited to herald the new creed with the zeal of disciples. Unfortunately, quite disparate images were conjured up as to the form it might take and little was done to dispel the notion that the millennium would follow quickly in its wake. Whilst there would be no great disagreement with the concept of corporate management being the key to the development of more comprehensive and rational decision making, the practice is conditioned totally by the style of management adopted by the chief executive and his management team. As there were disparate images built in anticipation, so there will be differences in practice. People make systems work and any attempt to formalise a corporate management system is both dangerous and unrealistic. The requirement to develop a corporate style has presented difficulties for officials as acute as those for councillors. A lifetime of working in a highly departmentalised system cannot readily be cast aside to assume a wider role in the management of the authority's affairs. The primary loyalty towards the department can so easily conflict with the requirement to recognise and appreciate the other service needs, especially in a time of financial stringency.

The relationship between chief officers and members, especially Chairmen, places new demands on the integrity of the individual officer. On the one hand the chief officer is expected to enter into a partnership with his chairman in achieving political ambition, and at the same time he is expected to contribute to the reconciliation of plans with the resources likely to be made available - not necessarily compatible objectives. Likewise, the chief executive as leader of the team and members of the Executive Office in support of the chief executive are required to maintain a careful balance within the team and also between the service departments and the centre. This need to counter balance is of fundamental importance in allaying the natural antipathy of elected members towards the activities of the management team.

The relationship, or more accurately the disputes, between the regions and the districts have captured the attention of the media and have tended to call in question the capacity of elected members to work in harmony with each other. These disputes have centred mainly around the so-called concurrent functions and no doubt objective observers find grounds for criticism of local government. However, the responsibility for this unfortunate arrangement must be assumed by the central government designers of the Local Government (Scotland) Act of 1973. It could only fall to someone so remote from reality and thus totally ignorant of the consequences to place a duty on one authority and a power on another. In practice the remaining pressure points on concurrent functions are mostly around the periphery of regional affairs and by definition away from the central area of decision making. The problems sometimes appear to be

22

intractable but the effect on the provision of major services is minimal and could be regarded as more of a surface irritation than a terminal disease. There is an interdependence between regions and districts brought about by the requirement to work closely in the planning field and and there are convincing arguments in favour of separating the strategic and the development planning roles. Undoubtedly this interdependence will bring the two levels of authority into conflict from time to time but it is suggested that the process of reconciliation may better serve the public interest.

It may be that 'tiers are tripe' as the **Scotsman** so delicately puts it. Time will tell and the earlier mention of the misplacement of responsibility for housing suggests that it may be sooner than later. However it is in the area of relations with central government that the greatest disappointment over reorganisation has arisen.

Lord Wheatley said - "From the practical point of view we have come to the conclusion that the kinds of control exercised by central government have in total a damaging effect on the independence and initiative of local authorities. We do not see how this situation can go on without casting doubt on the value of local government as an institution. For this reason we have been at pains to create a structure in which local government can be much stronger and in which its working relationship with central government can be altogether different from what it is now". That is still the practical point of view but if anything central government has tightened its grip on local government. It may be that the parlous state of the national economy requires exceptional discipline on the part of the public service but it is unfortunate that central government has chosen to act unilaterally in controlling the level of expenditure. Undoubtedly there is confusion between central and local government over the role each has to play in the control of local government spending. It is axiomatic that central government includes the costs of local services in its financial plans but rarely, if ever, is local government afforded the opportunity to contribute at the planning stage. As a result local government is constantly left on the receiving end of policies which through experience they know to be impractical to implement. Central government is often driven to the mistaken conclusion that local government is incapable of putting its house in order. The difficulty is compounded by the tendency on the part of central government to underestimate the resource implications of new legislation. This uncertainty over responsibility has led central government to intervene more and more in setting standards for local government and in controlling spending programmes. A continuation of the policy of intervention would question the relevance of an elaborate two level structure designed to safeguard local democracy.

It falls to central government to control the share of the nation's resources devoted to the public service and local government can offer no challenge to that responsibility. It is at the next stage of resource planning that scope exists for a new arrangement to provide local government with the sought after opportunities to use local initiative and to hold themselves accountable to the electorate. The expectation within local government was one of an emerging and rewarding partnership, each contributing skills, and knowledge to the greater benefit of the public service. Alas, not so. Local government was publicly reprimanded by government and left exposed to the rates furore in 1975, some of which was caused by changes in government grant policy and much of it by inflation and inescapable inherited commitments. Local government deeply resented the public hostility fanned by those reprimands and it will take time and effort to build the new relationship so earnestly desired by local government. Perhaps the Layfield report on local government finance will provide the focus in the search for a new solution.

If Ministers and senior civil servants genuinely desire to co-operate, and there are signs that they do, more deliberate attempts must be made to develop the partnership concept to the stage where those who are planning are in close contact with those who are required to implement. It is a valid criticism of the present arrangement that senior civil servants have little or no experience of the management of services and conversely senior local government officials have little knowledge or experience of national planning systems. A new forum for the exchange of experience is required in addition to the two way channel which exists between central government and the Convention of Scottish Local Authorities.

Mention of the Convention highlights one of the outstanding achievements in Scottish local government and a credit to the judgement and good sense of regional and district councils throughout Scotland. The creation of a single association dedicated to providing a focal point for the discussion of matters affecting local government strengthens the authority of the service as a whole. The challenge has been taken up but it will be some time before the full potential of the Convention as an instrument of influence is realised. Members and officers of the constituent authorities must recognise the need to devote more effort and resource to the achievement of the accepted aims. The secretariat must be provided with a research capability equal to the task of equipping the members to safeguard the interests of local democracy. The Convention must be effective and seen to be the natural counterbalance to the influence of the proposed Scottish Assembly.

And what of the future? Scotland is confronted with the prospect of an elected assembly having responsiblity for legislation devolved from Westminster and the question does arise as to the future place of local government following that arrangement. The main argument supporting devolution is one of allowing the Scottish people a greater say over affairs which vitally affect their lives. The same argument has been used to defend local democracy and the three levels adopted - region, district and community councils - are designed to ensure that government does not become remote from the people it seeks to serve. Those principles are in line with current thinking at the grass roots and it is important that they be upheld when the relationship between the Assembly and local government is worked out. Arguments are being advanced in favour of the Assembly assuming certain executive responsibilities in addition to the legislative role it will be required to perform. The centralist approach is attractive to those who see the transfer of the major local government functions to the

Assembly as a neat way of removing a heavy financial burden currently placed on ratepayers. Also in a simplistic way the manoeuvre is regarded as doubly attractive in that conveniently it appears to remove a tier of local government in the process. Lord Wheatley dealt convincingly with the case for a strong viable local government and it is no longer necessary to rehearse the argument in favour of its continued existence. The transfer of major local authority functions to the Assembly could be regarded as the antithesis of that argument. Experience suggests that in certain service areas e.g. social work and education, a constant striving for uniformity through imposed national standards, blunts initiative and sometimes misdirects resources away from those most in need. It is the defined role of local authorities to be the principal providers of service to the public and to be sensitive to the needs of local people. There is an added repsonsibility on regions to influence national policies through strategic plans. This is a period of rapid change in Scotland and many of its great institutions are under challenge as never before. The relevance of local democracy, it seems, must again be part of that challenge. It may be however, that the issue will be settled by the electorate themselves as there is no evidence to suggest that the people in Highland or Strathclyde will be any more prepared to accept local services from Edinburgh than they are to allow legislative arrangements to remain in Westminster.

The Reorganised Health Service

D.Hunter

There are as many definitions of health and disease as there are societies. In the 18th century men finally jettisoned the punitive and exorcist remedies and nostrums of the medieval pharmacopaeia. In the 19th century a new orthodoxy was founded when medicine — institutionalised in the hospital and laboratory — made it its business to prevent, arrest or mitigate the effects of disease. That orthodoxy is now in crisis. We must decide whether to continue to pour ever more resources into the rigidly hierarchical, technologically sophisticated and exceedingly expensive medical machine or try to create a "health-promoting" society. The recent reorganisation of the health service in Scotland gives reason to hope that we can break the bonds of current orthodoxies and develop a new, more adequate system of health care organisation.

The first point to make, with regard to the development of health services in Britain, is that it has never been anything but a desperate uphill struggle. No one who has read the history of the 19th century health pioneers can doubt that the struggles of Chadwick, Simon, Florence Nightingale and others, against the inherited order of things, and against the "Defenders of the Filth", were both prolonged and bitter. In this century, was there not a moment in the history of the psycho-analytical movement when the **police** were invoked as the proper means of getting rid of the Freudian heresy? The fact is that health services, like health itself, have always had to be fought for. As Bevan said: "Governments claiming health services for their own are claiming medals won in battles they have lost."

We are regaled with rumours and alarms about the current crisis in the NHS. No doubt it serves the purposes of different interest groups within the health care system to exaggerate the extent of any crisis that exists, as well as to suggest that it is an entirely new phenomenon. Some sensible comments on this issue can be found in the booklet "Health, Money and the National Health Service", which was published earlier this year by the Unit for the Study of Health Policy at Guy's Hospital. In so far as there is a crisis in the NHS, it is probably true to say that there has always been a crisis in health care in Britain.

In the past the crisis was a crisis of production, a crisis of **gross** shortages. Today the crisis is a crisis of distribution, a crisis of **relative** shortages. In short, what was a crisis of necessity and of constraint is now a crisis of choice and of priorities in a context of rising expectations and limited resources. In the age of the Poor Law, the classic equation, needs minus resources equals public health, was true in the most brutal, unqualified and absolute fashion. In the 19th century the right of health services to exist even on the periphery of society, as quasi-charitable entities, had to be painfully established. It was precisely because in the 19th century health services were not seen as part of the serious business of society, but rather as an affair of humanitarianism and Christian compassion, that they were left untouched by the new managerial and financial techniques which were beginning to dominate the industrial scene

Today the health care crisis not only involves infinitely more sophisticated and complex questions of ethics and priorities, but also has become a central issue in the affairs of the country; but it is the same crisis in a new form. Like other countries in the Western world, we in the UK have been subject, since the end of the Second World War, to a continuing crisis concerning the provision and organisation of health care. In Scotland, as in Britain generally, our first aim was to put health care on a systematic basis. Since the 1947 NHS (Scotland) Act was part of a general programme of nationalisation involving the railways, coal, gas and steel manufacturing, it reflected stable state, rational-efficient assumptions. One such assumption was Beveridge's maxim, that a health service would "diminish disease by prevention and cure", and ultimately it resulted, not so much in real health service , as in a mechanistic **sickness** service.

The 1948 Health Service was pre-eminently an aggregate of separate entities, artificially brought together into a single overall package. But it was not "born without ever having been conceived" and, in reality, the 1948 package was a good deal less rational and tidy than it appeared to be.

For all its imperfections, the 1948 model of the health service marked a turning point, in that it made health care available to the whole population without financial barriers and at the same time staked a continuing claim for resources for health care right at the centre of the governmental decision-making process. Moreover, in the years following upon its introduction, there was a substantial rationalisation through measures of make-do-and-mend of health care provision throughout the country. In

NATIONAL HEALTH SERVICE 1948–1974
ORGANISATION CHART

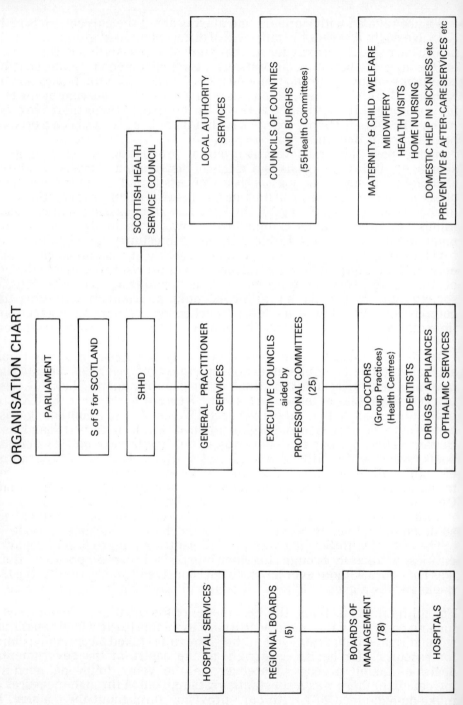

PARLIAMENT

S of S for SCOTLAND

SHHD

SCOTTISH HEALTH SERVICE COUNCIL

HOSPITAL SERVICES

REGIONAL BOARDS (5)

BOARDS OF MANAGEMENT (78)

HOSPITALS

GENERAL PRACTITIONER SERVICES

EXECUTIVE COUNCILS aided by PROFESSIONAL COMMITTEES (25)

DOCTORS (Group Practices) (Health Centres)

DENTISTS

DRUGS & APPLIANCES

OPTHALMIC SERVICES

LOCAL AUTHORITY SERVICES

COUNCILS OF COUNTIES AND BURGHS (55 Health Committees)

MATERNITY & CHILD WELFARE
MIDWIFERY
HEALTH VISITS
HOME NURSING
DOMESTIC HELP IN SICKNESS etc
PREVENTIVE & AFTER-CARE SERVICES etc

particular, although inequalities which are becoming increasingly difficult to justify still remain, key specialist skills were distributed more evenly than had ever been the case in the past.

1948-1974: The Search for Efficiency

After its inception in 1948 the evolution of the NHS, like the evolution of most complex systems, was mainly incremental and was only partly co-ordinated. The fact is that the stable state assumptions, on which it had been based, proved to be completely erroneous. Far from stabilising, the cost of health care escalated as the solution to one problem generated ten new ones. In consequence, since it had no strategy for coping with change, the 1948 model dealt with its problems by "putting on superfluous fat".

Only a few years after **Background and Blueprint** had given the new service its blessing, the Guillebaud Committee, with the help of Titmuss and Abel-Smith, pointed out that there was no level of health care which could be considered adequate, in any final sense. Indeed, with rising expectations and new advances in medicine, costs would be difficult to contain. Clearly Beveridge had been wrong to suggest that the new service would soon "pay its way". Clearly, too, when one considers the growing burden on the NHS at the present time, Mr Ian Mikardo, MP, had been wrong to say, in 1949, that the NHS had "made us into a healthy nation".

The Guillebaud Committee could see no remedy for the dilemma it had uncovered apart from the remedy of increased efficiency — and increased efficiency, involving a change of emphasis from administrative and procedural regularity to more dynamic managerial considerations, and from **fiscal,** or bookkeeping accountability, to **process** accountability — that is accountability in terms of value for money — became the watchword. But the collapse of the old certainties, and the existence of something like a vacuum of central leadership (the governmental machine, particularly in the pre-Fulton period, did not find it easy to adapt overnight to a managerial role), produced a situation of "disjointed incrementalism", in which there was no possibility of reconciling creativity and order. Central control was either arbitrary or non-existent and development on the periphery was inevitably hit or miss.

It was during the sixties, above all, that the NHS developed in an incrementalist and unco-ordinated fashion. In response to pressures from different groups within it, each of which set up a clamour for more resources, the service expanded. At the same time they often as not called for a "Health Service Beeching", who would be able to cut back on the "inefficient" expenditure of the other sectors. In the operational sphere, this system of "mutual partisan adjustment" generated ideas of multi-disciplinary functional management which led to the emergence of specialised nursing, administrative, works and hotel departments, not to speak of comprehensive medical divisions. At the same time the emphasis on operational efficiency within these functional departments resulted in an influx of work study, O. and M. and other efficiency experts. By 1973 the health service employed no fewer than 10,000 staff in new management services units, at an estimated annual cost of £6 million — a five or six-fold increase in the number of such workers compared with the early sixties.

In its own self-adjusting way the NHS had become big business. Spending in Scotland alone in 1973-74, the last year before reorganisation, was £341,538,000 compared with £117,077,000 ten years before that — a real increase in health service expenditure of about 60%. In spite of all these developments, however, and although the health care system in the UK had a better record in terms of value for money than many other systems of health care, it became clear, during the sixties, that managerial efficiency at the operational level would not be enough to bring escalating costs under control. This situation was a prime determinant in the formulation of government policy in the late sixties, when a more fundamental solution to the difficulties and dilemmas of the NHS was proposed.

It was now accepted that, in order to resolve the difficulties which the health service was encountering, both in regard to rising costs and in regard to its inability to meet the growing needs of the elderly, the mentally ill and the mentally handicapped, structural reorganisation, involving clinical integration and managerial unification, must be superimposed on the existing structure. As indicated, reorganisation had two basic aims which were not necessarily compatible. Indeed, whether these aims could be made compatible depended on the respective priorities accorded to them. On the one hand a restructured health service, with a built-in planning system, could simply be ''more of the same'', could simply be the final instalment of the efficiency and effectiveness era. On the other hand reorganisation could be regarded as an attempt to eliminate the mismatch between what the NHS was doing and what it should be doing. Given the change in the pattern of illness from acute infections to chronic conditions and from the disease men die of to those they have to live with, some change in the NHS was obviously needed. The 1948 NHS had been an illness service. Was it now time to create a **health** service which would maintain whole populations in health and which would give priority to care in the community instead of to cure in hospital?

The New Service

In England it is clear that what mattered in the period between 1968 and 1971 was **managerial control.** The central objective of the new service was to be effective management. In his introduction to the Consultative Document, which was issued in May 1971 and which foreshadowed the English White Paper and the subsequent Bill, the then Secretary of State Sir Keith Joseph, saw the management part of the package as his special contribution and, in describing the proposals, said that their essence, and their basic difference from earlier proposals, was the emphasis which they placed on effective management.

In Scotland a more imaginative stance, which may have reflected the oft-repeated views of the CMO, Sir John Brotherston, was adopted. The remedy, even for escalating costs, was seen to lie less in managerial control than in a basic reorientation of the health service. Perhaps the first essential was to break away from the vicious circle of high technology

HEALTH SERVICE ORGANISATION : SCOTLAND

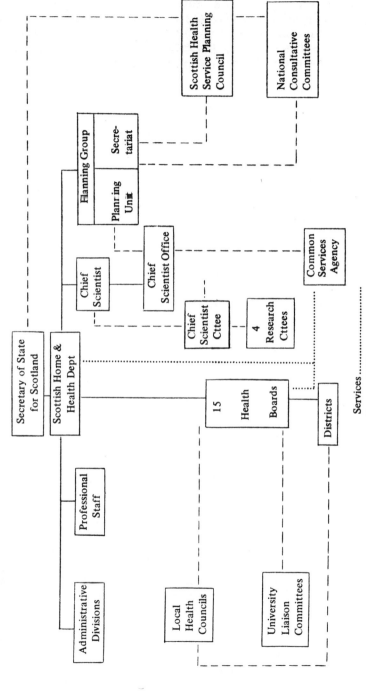

medicine and from Tudor Hart's "Inverse Law of Health Care". Whatever may have been the approach elsewhere, reorganisation in Scotland was not simply an attempt on the part of the government to regain control of a runaway health service through policies of increased centralisation. In fact the new structure is clearly centralised in certain respects; but it is much more than that.

As the organisation chart demonstrates, there has been a considerable degree of streamlining and centralisation. The reduction of 56 local health committees, 25 executive councils, five regional boards and 65 boards of management to a mere 15 Health Boards speaks for itself. However, it is the participative aspects of the new service, namely the Common Services Agency, the Scottish Health Service Planning Council, the National Consultative Committees, the Local Health Councils, the new ombudsman and the consensus style of management represented by Area and District Executive Groups that are crucial. These are to be the real growth points of the new NHS in Scotland, if it is to move in the direction of a paitent-centred service, backed up by a professional organisation.

The emphasis in Scotland was **clinical** not managerial. Reorganisation had two aims and those aims were stated in the following order:

(1) to integrate the personal health services "round the patient" — an old dream of Aneurin Bevan –by providing interrelated services to cope with interrelated problems, and to develop, so far as possible, a preventive community-based system of health care; and

(2) to provide these integrated caring and treatment services within a unified but supportive system of management, operating in the context of a flexible, anticipatory and participative planning process which would have a "cumulative" impact on the future development of the NHS in Scotland. This new approach to the health care crisis, involving a change of emphasis from efficiency and effectiveness to long-term strategic considerations, and from **process,** to **programme** accountability, has immense potential. But the fact that the future of the NHS, like the future of other organisations and institutions, must increasingly be a man-made future also presents the health professions, health administrators and the community itself with daunting problems and responsibilities.

For a future-orientated health service, managerial models drawn from concepts of "top-down" authority are inappropriate. But the new concepts of organisation more appropriate to human service organisation came into good currency in the UK only in the period 1966-71. So it was probably inevitable that both in Scotland, and in England and Wales (where use was made not only of McKinsey and Co. but also of the neo-scientific management, "building-block", approach of the Brunel Health Service Research Unit), reliance was placed on conventional, industrial-bureaucratic models. But whereas this was deliberate in the south, it is likely that in Scotland it was a case of hierarchy **faute de mieux.** In any event, whether it is because Scotland is still a homogeneous society with good communications, or whether it is because the Scottish tradition of democratic humanism is still something to be reckoned with, the Scottish model of the reorganised NHS differed from the English and Welsh one by the extent to which it emerged as a participative model.

In England and Wales the bureaucratic structure of the new NHS was vigorously attacked before reorganisation and is now regarded by some commentators as a total mistake. In Scotland it is still possible to hope that Oliver Wendell Homes' famous remark to Harold Laski — never mind the **system,** tell me about the **insights** — can be adapted to meet the case of a formal structure which is not wholly congruent with the goals it has been set up to achieve but which is nevertheless redeemed by the incorporation of some imaginative participative mechanisms. Among these are the following:

(1) Local Health Councils (based on ideas first promulgated in the Wheatley Report and appearing in the reorganised NHS in England and Wales as "community health councils");

(2) the Common Services Agency;

(3) the National (and Local) Consultative Committees of the health care professions; and

(4) the Scottish Health Service Planning Council which is unique to Scotland and which advises the Secretary of State on the future development of the NHS in Scotland. It is a forum for shared decision-making, comprising, as it does, six senior administrative and professional officers of the Scottish Home and Health Department, and a representative from each of the 15 Health Boards and from each of the four medical schools in Scotland, all meeting under the impartial chairmanship of (at the present time) the Principal of Edinburgh University.

Given these participative mechanisms it is possible to believe that there is no going back in these matters and that we must work "in the interstices" of the technocracy in order to humanise it and make it more client-centred.

Still on this hopeful note, it can be said that the reorganised health service in Scotland at least has the potential to move fairly rapidly in the direction of a client-oriented service, based on **programme** accountability, which will involve us in developing, through the professional advisory system, not only comprehensive programmes of care for specific patient groups but also the cross-cutting service plans which will be necessary to meet the requirements of these programmes. The possibility exists, therefore, of a dramatic leap into the future. But in Scotland, too, one has misgivings lest the traditional elements in the new administrative structure should succeed in dragging the reorganised service screaming not merely into the pre-1948 era but actually into the 19th century. Instead of having been content to ask ourselves where we should be **going,** instead of having been content to "veer away from past failures", perhaps we should have given some thought to where, in the last quarter of the 20th century, we really ought to **be.**

It is too soon to say that, once again, we are driving into the future with the help of the rear mirror alone; but some of the problems and dilemmas which are now being encountered have an unmistakably familiar ring. They are certainly problems and dilemmas of dynamic conservatism, and of "fighting like mad to stay where we are", rather than problems and dilemmas of positive adaptation to new problems, new challenges, and new opportunities.

One could instance as examples of these all-too-familiar difficulties, the stresses even in Scotland (which has one tier fewer than England and Wales) between the different levels of the hierarchical management structure. Also there is a problem simply because it **is** a hierarchical structure, of the movement of administrators of quality towards the top of the pyramid. It is this upward movement which has produced a situation of "the administration with the hole". It is a forcible reminder that the relationship between the old Boards of Management and the Regional Boards was a **collateral** relationship rather than a superior-subordinate one. One could also mention the health-social work dichotomy, the communication problems which have arisen between Local Health Councils and Health Boards in some parts of the country and the rivalries of professionals and bureaucrats which are inherent in all hierarchical structures. There also seems to be a marked tendency to hark back to procedural regularity, when what is called for is increased flexibility, increased informality, and an increasing emphasis on the real goals of the health care system. To be sure, it may be too soon to say that these regressive tendencies are merely a temporary and, to some extent, a reassuring phenomenon. In a period of increasing complexity and change, dynamic conservatism has a key part to play in keeping the system from flying apart at the seams. One can only reiterate that there are participative mechanisms in the Scottish model, which make it possible for us to view the reorganised NHS not as our final destination but merely as a better starting point than the 1948 one ever was.

What the chrysalis of the new NHS can yet evolve into is an open system, or arena, of health care. One in which, once artificial authority barriers have been eroded, the tapping of our new potential for working together can begin to rank as the first priority. Is it possible to envisage a "negotiated order" in the health care system, with professionals acting in supportive ways in regard to other professionals in the multidisciplinary settings of health care teams? Can we envisage such health care teams interlocking with and supporting other teams, so that the periphery of the health care system starts knitting itself together into a series of flexible, "self-transforming networks"? Finally, can we envisage these peripheral, or operational, networks, however "shadowy" they may be in the first instance, being linked to, and even overlapping with, central supportive networks? If so, in time and in a cumulative way, we can begin to plan and co-ordinate networks not only of health services, but also of health related services like social work, housing and education.

Our hope must be that the momentum of change will carry us over some

34

of the reefs and shallows, and over some of the deeper gulfs and under-currents, which at present block our passage to the open sea, and that, before too long, we shall be able to achieve the sophisticated levels of provision which are now at least possible of attainment. All this having been achieved, however, will it actually constitute a real breakthrough? Or will it merely be yet another "veering away from past failures"? Will it still be a health service based on the question: "Where should we be **going**?" instead of on the question, "Where should we **be**?" Will it still be a health service that is concerned with negative, as distinct from, positive prevention and with our "limping" rather than with our "walking"?

Towards an Alternative Health Care Model

Merely to ask these questions is to open up new horizons and to suggest the need for a genuine reversal of perspectives, leading to an alternative model of health care. Health is not something we have had and lost. It is not something which can be restored to us by hospitals and clinics. We do not have a health industry in the sense that we can manufacture health. As a recent Scottish Home and Health Department publication said, "It is a paradox of the present system that so much is spent on ineffective cure while so little is done to encourage the public in general to improve its own health" (1976). Health, in short, has less to do with health services than with life-chances and life-styles. It is the life-styles of individuals in society, and the life-style of society as a whole, that are decisive.

It has been said that modern medicine is on the edge of a Copernican Revolution and that doctors are awaiting a single turn of thought, comparable to knowing that the earth is not flat, before medicine can take a new direction.

Self-help, self-health, the community itself as doctor do these concepts indicate the **real** way ahead? Of course, community development at this level of intensity is not a realistic expectation at present but perhaps it is not too far over the horizon, particularly if one is prepared to accept what Julia Abrahamson has said in "A Neighbourhood Finds Itself": "In the people of every community everywhere there is a vast untapped potential, almost limitless energy and resources which can be released for community betterment. Freeing that potential and channelling it into constructive citizen action can provide a powerful source of strength in the saving of our cities and the regeneration of the nation."

The social anthropologists have described societies in which community care was a major ingredient in health care and it seems that, once again, community involvement is the Archimedes point giving us the leverage on the world which we need for the next great advance. Industrialisation destroyed our small village communities with their intricate community support systems. In doing so it also introduced concepts of prevention in terms of which disease could be averted or avoided since it was no longer a visitation or a punishment for some breach of taboo or sin or transgression. But the rationalistic proponents of negative prevention, and of a "sanitated society", went too far in proposing that disease could be totally eradicated by "health services".

Health promotion policies and policies of positive prevention aim at integrating both of these approaches, first, by recreating the village on a national (or global) scale and, secondly, by reinforcing, through the statutory health care system, the potential of the community, under conditions of post-industrialism, for self-help and self-health.

It is ironical that, after all the agonised to-ing and fro-ing, both in Scotland and in the rest of the UK, about the reorganisation of the NHS — a reorganisation which it is to be hoped will not be found to have saddled the community with an even more technocratic system of health care than that which existed between 1948 and 1974 — the real clue to the future is almost certainly to be found in those developments in health care which are now being pioneered in the Third World.

The focus of this paper is on the reorganisation of the NHS in Scotland. Yet "society itself is the real patient" and health services do not, in fact, manufacture health. Ninety-five per cent of our improved health over the last 200 years has come, not from medical intervention (which has contributed 5 per cent or thereabouts and that only since the thirties) but from general social advance. So it may now be permissible to speculate about the **deorganisation** and debureaucratisation of health care.

Health services are an indispensable (although increasingly costly and, in some respects, increasingly dangerous) **resource.** But, central to the quality of life in modern society, is the concept of self-health in the context of a health-promoting society (Unit for the Study of Health Policy, 1976). The implications of this concept for a materialistic, divisive and inegalitarian society are now the "strategic factor". In industrial psychology Herzberg has distinguished between the "hygiene factors", without which men cannot work at all, and the "motivating factors", which inspire them to give of their best. Ingeniously equating Herzberg's "hygiene factors" with the role of hospital-based health services and his "motivating factors" with community self-help and concepts of self-health, Michael Wilson has written a book called "Health is for People" (1975). Even more apposite perhaps, and certainly more germane to the theme of this paper, is the title of a recent WHO publication (1976) which reports on some of the remarkable self-help advances in health care which have taken place through techniques of "simplified medicine" in the Third World in communities so apathetic and "spiritless" that they often seemed beyond recovery. Conveying, according to Morris Carstairs, "something new and important, and in plain language", this book is called "Health By the People".

We do not really have a new health service in Scotland. What we have is a health service which is constantly evolving and which, at the present time is in a state of fairly rapid transition and development. It is impossible to predict — and it is really anyone's guess — how political devolution, if it becomes a reality, will retard or accelerate the processes of deorganisation and debureaucratisation of health care, which have been mentioned above.

Following upon the administrative deconcentration which took place

36

earlier this century, there is a certain logic in political devolution; and, in terms of classical political theory, such devolution **should** have a beneficial impact on the administration of all the services for which the Scottish Office is responsible. Equally, however, if one may be the devil's advocate, political influence on the administration of health services has often had baneful consequences. What we must hope, however, is that it is not macro-politics of the party-political type but rather micro-politics of the community type — direct contact with the patient and the community through "participative", as distinct from "representative", institutions — that will constitute the lifeblood of a health care system. Nor can any of the political parties maintain that, in the event of devolution, their chief aim would be to "de-politicise" health care in Scotland, because "taking the NHS out of poltics" merely means taking it out of the other man's politics and bringing it into one's own .

Still in the role of the devil's advocate, one could go further and suggest that the attempt to find a 19th century macro-political solution for Scotland's present-day economic and social problems could, in itself, represent the single most vivid manifestation, on the current scene, of dynamic conservatism in action. The historian, Maitland, saw the relationship of Scotland and England, from the 16th century on, as a dynamic one, involving both increasing economic centralisation and increasing cultural decentralisation. It is certainly important to appreciate that issues of centralisation and decentralisation can be only too easily over-simplified. The impact of devolution on the Scottish NHS, as on other areas of our national life, **could** be negative rather than forward-looking.

Early in 1976 Archbishop Thomas   Winning of Glasgow published a statement reaffirming the views of the Bishops of Scotland. His statement was called **The Positive Value of Catholic Education.** Archbishop Winning's statement elicited a strong response , after W McKechin Vice Chairman of Strathclyde's Education Committee took issue with the Bishop Brian Gill, an advocate,   supported him. Both wrote in the Times Educational Supplement (Scotland). Father Anthony Ross, writing in **Question** also took issue with the Bishops statement. We reprint the essence of the various statements here with a preface by Colin MacLean. Editor of the TES (S):

Education in a sectarian society

several views

preface

C.MacLean

To my mind, no debate of this century in Scottish education is more important than that about Roman catholic schools, for this debate embraces all the major questions about the power that Government does, could or should have in determining the character of education - its diversity, its discipline, its content, its style. No obstacle to all-inclusive, uniform comprehensivisation has been greater than that of the Roman Catholic schools. The RC Church is not the national church. There are strongly opposed views about separate RC schools among members of the RC community and also within the national established Church of Scotland (for some Protestants feel strongly that the RC schools should survive!) also the Labour Party is incapable of achieving even a semblance of unity on the subject. Personally I am glad that the RC schools provide so intractable a problem because they ensure continuing and potentially productive tension over the issue of the right of choice for any religious or cultural group, for members of the teaching profession, for parents, and eventually (I hope) for pupils. Pupils of what age? - the question is at the heart of the most fundamental question in education.

'The Positive Value of Catholic Education' Archbishop Winning

Catholic education has the opportunity to be unique and the greater responsibility to be contemporary and open.

Unique, because it offers well defined religious truths and values as the basis for living and learning.

Contemporary, for it provides the young with Catholic insights into the many problems facing individuals and society today.

Open, for although it offers a Catholic outlook, it does not condemn other points of view, or take up positions against them - but aims at using acquired knowledge, skills and habits of mind and heart for effective Christian service to the whole community, teaching mutual understanding, respect of others, and genuine tolerance.

Catholic education aims at producing men and women capable of taking their place in society as educated adult Christians. Modern trends make this kind of education more necessary than ever. The Church is too experienced in education to be misled into thinking, like many education theorists today, that the teaching of a commitment to a specific religious faith is incompatible with academic freedom. Catholic education unashamedly aims at locating the message of Christ proclaimed by the Church at the very heart of the entire syllabus, curriculum and life of the school community.

Yet, the 1972 Report commissioned by the Secretary of State for Scotland on "Moral and Religious Education in Scottish (non-denominational) Schools" has this to say about the current aims of religious education.

"But religious education is no longer aimed at producing assent to any particular set of propositions or commitment to one particular faith . . ."

and again

"The teacher is not there to convince pupils of specific religious beliefs (far less to make them learn them)." (cf. pp. 68-69).

Surely Catholic education has more to offer than this. The Catholic Church rejects this theory of religious education for it is based on a false concept of the very nature of the Church and the role of evangelisation which is the task of all committed Christians. Indeed, in the light of such a basic divergence all other acknowledged defects in our educational system, from shortage of teachers to cramped accommodation, are of secondary importance. The Christian child fits into a Christian philosophy. Real dialogue can only exist between people who have convictions, between people who know what they are and what they want. It is tragic to realise that genuine Christian education has been so compromised by modern secular theories upheld at times even by Christians.

Our idea of community has nothing in common with the ghetto mentality. Catholic education is not institutional protection. We would be failing the Church were we to regard Catholic education merely as an attempt to hold onto what we have. Individually and as a community we accept our responsibilities in society. But to be open to the world does not mean to conform to the world. It is one of the great advantages of an age in which unbelief speaks out that faith can speak out too; that if falsehood opposes truth, truth can oppose falsehood.

Some Catholic parents have their children educated at non-denominational schools despite the existence of a Catholic school in their locality. I doubt if any of these parents have any serious criticism of Catholic education in its theory or presentation, but in the light of what has been said above, are they fulfilling their duty to their children? Do they realise that they are depriving their children of the support of a Catholic school community, staff, pupils and chaplain? Are they putting social values before spiritual values?

The Catholic home is not a substitute for the Catholic school, nor is the Catholic school a substitute for the Catholic home. In such a complex society as ours the Catholic home needs the support of the Catholic school to ensure that knowledge and understanding of the faith grow apace with intellectual development. Similarly, the Catholic school requires the backing of good example from the Catholic home. Together they make a formidable team; apart, they leave gaps which can never be filled.

Every Catholic child has the right to a Catholic education and every Catholic parent has the duty to acknowledge that right. Indeed, each member of the Catholic community has some role to play, especially in those parts of the country where there are no Catholic schools. Here the contribution of parents, clergy and lay educators assumes even greater importance.

'A Matter of Public Concern'
W.J.McKechin

The natural reaction of most people to Archibishop Winning's recent statement on Roman Catholic schools made on behalf of all the RC bishops in Scotland and handed out at Catholic churches throughout the length and breadth of Scotland to each and every Catholic who attended mass, is that it deals with an internal matter that is the concern of Catholics only and none of their affair. However, it cannot be so readily dismissed, as Catholic schools are not solely the property and prerogative of Catholic Church. They are state schools, which as the law states "shall be held, maintained and managed by the education authorities as public schools". They are thus a matter of public concern and cannot be exempted from debate.

It is no secret that Catholic schools have in recent times been coming under increasing criticism on various counts, mainly but not wholly from within the Catholic Church. There has been the growing difficulty of staffing them with Catholics, so that more and more they are having to be buttressed up by non-Catholic teachers; but even at that they are still the most chronically understaffed of schools. There is growing disquiet among parents about their performance. A much smaller proportion of pupils complete a full secondary course in RC secondaries than in non-denominational schools.

On the religious side, some Catholic parents have begun to question if Catholic schools are doing the job they are supposed to do, namely instruct Catholic children in their Catholic faith, and also on a much wider issue to question if in this ecumenical age separate Catholic schools, with their inbuilt inward approach and separateness, provide the most fitting way to instil or practise the Christian precept of brotherly love in the true Christian spirit of all men being brothers regardless of race, colour, class or creed .

The statement has thus primarily been made to counter an existing situation and this is evident by the defensive tone that resounds throughout the document. Although in the past ten years much has changed in both the religious and educational worlds, it is almost a repeat of the pastoral letter on Catholic schools, written by Bishop Thomson, the present RC bishop of Motherwell, and issued on behalf of the RC bishops of Scotland in November 1966, except for a few differences in detail and presentation. The substance is almost the same and except for a few changes in emphasis its argument is almost identical: the argument is obviously theological but developed in a way peculiar to clerics and appealing only to clerics.

It is unlikely to have any more impact than the previous pastoral letter, as it in no ways deals with or tries to answer the problems that beset many Catholic parents, anxious to be true to their religious beliefs, but equally anxious for the welfare and future of their offspring.

The whole statement exudes an air of unawareness of the nature and magnitude of the difficulties under which Catholic schools labour and of the

41

quality of education, both secular and religous which is provided in them, pointing to inadequate briefing. This might have been avoided if advice had not been sought in quarters which seem to be more concerned in purveying reassurance than in conveying unpalatable truths.

Many of these unpalatable truths are to be found in two well discussed publications which the Scottish Education Department have issued in the past few years, **Secondary Schools - Staffing Survey, 1970** and **Secondary School Staffing,** where statistics relating to the qualifications, age distribution and supply of Catholic teachers are revealed in all their melancholy inadequacy. Although clearly, if somewhat tersely presented, the implications of these statistics may not be immediately apprenehded by those who are not professional educationists, but there must surely be sufficient of those amongst the Catholic community able to outline their full significance and consequences.

Only someone unaware of the true situation could as the statement does term the shortage of Catholic teachers in Catholic secondaries as temporary, when for nigh on 60 years, that is ever since Catholic schools came under the state unbrella in 1918, Catholic schools have never been able to operate without non-Catholic teachers.

There have always been some non-Catholic teachers on their staffs, but in the past few years the situation has worsened in that the percentage of non-Catholic teachers has continued to increase at a rate which shows no sign of abating and which, if it continues as at present, will in a few years ensure that most teachers in Catholic schools will be non-Catholics, a situation which will make it near impossible to claim a unique Catholic atmosphere for Catholic schools or to describe them as "communities sharing the same religious truths and moral values".

One also can only be grossly misinformed to maintain "we should not be discouraged or misled into thinking that academic standards in Catholic schools suffer in comparison with those in non-denominational schools". It is true that as public schools the standards set by education authorities are the same for both sets of schools, RC and non-denominational, but their attainment of these standards certainly differs as indicated by the fact that the percentage of pupils in Catholic Schools who attain three or more passes at Higher grade is little more than half the corresponding percentage in non-denominational schools.

In criticising the Millar report, it is difficult to know what meaning the statement assigns to the phrase "academic freedom" when it states: "The church is too experienced in education to be misled into thinking, like many education theorists today, that the teaching of a commitment to a specific religious faith is incompatible with academic freedom". It can scarcely be the normally accepted one where "academic freedom" means the freedom of an educational policy and devise its own curricula without being subject to any external pressure or interference: a meaning in no way limited to a religious context.

Nor in this respect is academic freedom the argument that educationists would advance. Rather they would argue that religious education is not concerned with commitment but with insight, that its

42

purpose is to unfold the relationship between religion and man in all aspects, historical, mystical, metaphysical, moral, ethical, psychological, ritualistic, so that the believer, regardless of his commitment can have a deeper appreciation of what he believes in. On the other hand to limit a person's religious education to a recital of the beliefs and practices of a particular religion is to abort the possibility of his or her religious development.

The statement hinges on its opening phrase: "Christ's mission is our mission, Christ's message is our message. And Catholic education is an essential expression of our mission", a statement which no committed Catholic would deny, even those who send their children to non-Catholic schools. What is at question is not Catholic education but Catholic schools, from which follows the corollary "are Catholic schools necessary for Catholic education?"

Throughout the statement education is confused with schools. But education existed long before schools and will continue to exist long after schools depart. So also will Catholic education. The Roman Catholic church has existed for almost two thousand years: compulsory universal schooling has only recently celebrated its centenary.

It is disturbing to think that a church with a tradition of transmitting its faith with undiminished fervour for centuries through generation after generation of illiterate peasants now claims it can only be done propped up by a school system subsisting on public funds, a claim all the more damning when one can see all around other churches, none of whose resources bear comparison, doing it successfully and unaided.

How did the Catholic Church manage in the nineteen centuries preceding universal schooling? How did it fulfil Christ's mission? Perhaps because it exercised a more energetic witness. Perhaps because then it really was what it now claims it is, a teaching church. The church is where commitment should begin, where it should be nurtured and where it should come to fruition Commitment should not be hived off to a vehicle which is incapable of coping with it. Not only is it ruining the education of Catholics, but it is destroying the very fabric of their church.

'Faithful in spite of discouragement'
Brian Gill

My reaction to Archbishop Winning's statement on Roman Catholic education is one of enthusiasm. The statement or to be accurate the restatement, is timely, well expressed and positive in its emphasis. It's moderate but uncompromising tone is typical of its author whose impact on Scottish religious life has already been considerable and will I am sure, undoubtedly increase.

NotwithstandingMr W. J. McKechin's hostility towards the statement (February 13), there are, I think, one or two matters on which I agree with him.

I readily agree that the existence of separate Catholic schools within the state system is a proper matter of public concern and public debate. Unlike Mr McKechin, I would be surprised to hear anyone argue the contrary.

Mr McKechin is well founded in what I take to be his impression that many Catholic parents are now questioning some of the assumptions of the hierarchy, and little wonder. They, unlike their pastors, have a direct personal interest. They have perfectly respectable social and economic aspirations for their children and, rightly or wrongly, they are doubtful whether the Catholic sector of the public education system can fulfil them.

Although they persevere in their support of the Catholic schools, there is much to discourage them.There is the complacentassumption by certain of their bishops that the Catholic representation on regional education committees should always be clergymen, a view which is all too typical of the clerical view of the laity in the Scottish Church.

Such parents are discouraged when dissenting Catholic clergymen publicly attack the idea of Catholic education without there being any public rebuttal from the hierarchy. They are discouraged by the craven reluctance of the clergy to engage in public controversy on the question of separate schools or to intervene on their behalf in specific local issues, such as staffing, affecting the religious welfare of their children. They are discouraged by the variable consistency with which individual prelates support the Catholic colleges of education.

They are discouraged by the inadequate representation of parents, and the extravagent representation of teachers, on the Catholic Education Commission, a body directly appointed by the hierarchy. They are discouraged, too, by the commission itself which is unimaginative in its ambitions, amateurish in its performance and hindered in much of its work by a leaden preoccupation with the narrow career concerns of the Catholic teaching profession.

Despite all of this, however, most Catholic parents persevere in their support of Catholic schools because they see in them the best possible avenue in the modern world towards the attainment of the highest ideals of Christian education. They are fortified in this view by authoritative evidence about the state of religious education in the non-denominational schools. They see in their schools the only opportunity for an overtly Christian form of education, however imperfectly attained, because the non-denominational schools have long disclaimed such an ideal.

Christian education is not mere instruction in belief. At its best it is for teacher and pupil alike, a profound religious experience. To lead a young mind to the knowledge, understanding and love of God is no mean task. To participate in it is part of the sacred duty of Christian parenthood.

Such are the values of Christian education, and such are the values which Archbishop Winning's statement reasserts.

The problem which has characterised this debate over the years has certainly not been that of identifying the Catholic standpoint which, much to the indignation of its critics has remained constant and consistently expressed. Mr McKechin is absolutely right when he says of the statement that, when compared with the bishops' pastoral letter of 1966, "the substance is almost the same and except for a few changes in emphasis its argument is almost identical". I find it difficult to imagine what changes in the substance of the argument he would have preferred.

This, to my mind, is Mr McKechin's least profitable line of attack, because the presuppositions of the Catholic argument are such that its logic is unchanging.

To state the issue in this way leaves open, of course, all questions as to the practicability of implementing the Christian ideal within the Catholic school or the efficiency with which those schools are run. I would not deny that substantial criticisms, not necessarily those adopted by Mr McKechin, can be cogently advanced against the present system.

But the real issue is not faced in skirmishing over statistical data about staffing ratios and examination results. A much more fundamental propostion underlies Mr McKechin's argument, and that is that there ought not to be a group of schools kept separate on sectarian lines.

This is altogether a much worthier subject for debate, because it brings us to a consideration of the nature of education itself, of the place spirituality in the formation of the individual personality and of the rights and responsibilities of parent in the ethical and spiritual development of their children.

When the positive assertions of the Christian position on the issue are made, as in the statement, the alternatives must be examined and, since there are several, anyone seeking the abolition of the Catholic schools must disclose which alternative he supports, and, since he seeks to invert the status quo argue his justification of it.

These alternative solutions range from a candid support for the abolition of Christianity in public education to an idealistic but wholly naive belief that Christian reconciliation will flourish, despite the objective evidence of the Millar report, in a so-called integrated system, and at the other extreme to an acceptance of the vapid indifferentism that is the inevitable product of some ill-defined programme of non-committal religous studies.

Mr McKechin unhesitatingly adopts the latter solution, and it is in the glimpse of it which he permits us that the unsoundness of his position becomes clear. In his comment on the statement's reference to the Millar

45

report Mr McKechin reveals an alarming readiness to prefer the claims of the school over those of the home.

Citing with approval the arguments of some undefined body of educationists, he favours an educational order in which religious education is concerned not with commitment but with insight.

Such educationists, he says, "would argue that religious education is not concerned with commitment but with insight, that its purpose is to unfold the relationship between religion and man in all aspects, historical, mystical, metaphysical, moral, ethical, psychological, ritualistic, etc., so that the believer, regardless of his commitment, can have a deeper and more meaningful appreciation of what he believes in"; while on the other hand "to limit a person's religious education to a recital of the beliefs and practices of a particular religion is to abort the possibility of his or her religious development".

It is necessary to examine this line of argument in some detail because it would convince Mr McKechin and his supporters, whatever were the academic attainments of Catholic schools.

I dispute the assumption that commitment and insight are true alternatives. There is no reason why commitment to a clearly defined religious standpoint should necessarily deprive a child of insight into the general features of religion as a social phenomenon. I assert as a fact that that need not be and is not the effect of Catholic education. What evidence is there to the contrary?

I certainly dispute the assumption that Catholic education limits a child's religious education to a recital of the beliefs and practices of his religion. What evidence is there to support this assumption? And even if such a recital of beliefs and practices was the sum and substance of Catholic education (which is not the case) it by no means follows that the effect of it is to "abort" the possibility of the individual's religious development. Again, what evidence is there for such an assertion, and what does Mr McKechin mean by "religious development" in this argument?

Is it a maturing of a religious faith, in which case how can that be achieved in the young without instruction in the beliefs and practices of that religion?

Or does "religious development" contain, as I suspect, a further covert assumption, namely that it refers to a desired maturing out of any specific sectarian allegiance?

Anyone pretending to serious participation in this debate has to come clean about these assumptions, because they are by no means too obvious for argument, least of all when they are prefaced by such question-begging propositions as that "in this ecumenical age" separate Catholic schools have an "inbuilt inward approach to separateness".

Separateness from what? From Presbyterianism? Is that the predominant character of the non-denominational schools, and if it is, is separateness from it an impediment to ecumenism, particularly when the Protestant interpretation of ecumenism has consistently and understandably, emphasised its refusal to yield on fundamental beliefs?

Even in his assessment of the Catholic Church's mission, which he dismisses ,with regretable tastelessness, as that of "transmitting its faith ... through generation after generation of illiterate peasants", there is no respite from Mr McKechin's unfounded assumptions.

"The church" he says, "is where commitment should begin, where it should be matured and where it should come to fuition. Commitment should not be hived off to a vehicle which is incapable of coping with it". But here again Mr McKecnin misapprehends the nature of Christian education, for the school, like the home is part of the living church. It is part of an integrated system. It is not a substitute for either the church or the home.

Despite these strictures I do not wholly discount the value of Mr McKechin's contribution on the subject. His expression of view together with the more strident hostility of the media, must surely convince the Catholic hierachy of what they are up against. No one, so far as I am aware, has claimed that the abolition of the Catholic schools would mean the abolition of the Catholic Church in Scotland, but it would, in my view, gravely impair the church's mission.

If, therefore, it is the duty of the Catholic parent to support the separate system of Catholic schools (as the statement plainly asserts), such a parent is entitlted to ask what the hierarchy propose to do to help him in the performance of his duty.

Are they prepared to join the controversy at a political rather than a theological level? Are they prepared if need be, to marshal the votes of their flock to save the schools?

If not, what practical steps do they seriously ask the parents to take? And, above all, what practical proposals do they have in the short term for the academic improvement of the Catholic schools?

'Should the Schools be Integrated?'

Anthony Ross

A considerable number of people share the hope that specifically Roman Catholic schools will cease to exist in Scotland before long. The Catholic bishops on the other hand have recently re-affirmed their determination to defend the present system with all the strength they can muster, and claim to have support in their stand from the majority of Catholic parents. If the majority of parents do feel as strongly as the bishops claim then the question of integrating "Catholic" schools and "Protestant" schools is politically too explosive to handle, given the present delicate political balance and the size of the Catholic vote in certain areas of Scotland.

It is of course often forgetten that support for the existing system comes not only from Catholics but also from staunch members of other social or religious groups. There are, for example, those who fear the emergence of a monolithic state educational system which would ignore parental rights and assist the growth of totalitarian bureaucracy. They see the system of Catholic schools as a major bulwark of democratic freedom. Then there are members of other denominations who believe that Catholics are right to insist on the religious aspect of education and who feel that the Church of Scotland in particular has failed to resist the spread of secularism, through weakness of faith by letting religious instruction decline almost to vanishing point in many, if not most, schools.

The Catholic community is not as united on the schools question as it may seem in official pronouncements on the pages of the Catholic press. I received evidence of this personally after advocating some years ago, on a television programme, an integrated school system at least at secondary school level. Nevertheless Catholics have reason to be at least wary when intgration is discussed, for it is not as simple a matter as its advocates often seem to believe. Nor are they a single-minded group; their motives for wishing the disappearance of Catholic schools are indeed varied.

Some are in fact hostile to religious teaching of a doctrinal nature, whatever its source, and would elminiate it from schools altogether; or at most allow some form of comparative religious studies claiming to be objective, even scentific in character. Could the sort of teacher this supposes actually be found in sufficient numbers?

Others appear to see integration as the solution to the sort of sectarianism so tragically illustrated in extreme form in Northern Ireland. By concentrating on integration they can avoid for a time the historical, social and economic facts of a situation. But can integration work on a

48

general scale in somewhere like Northern Ireland unless there are already massive numbers of parents and teachers committed to making it work? Some appear to be playing devious ecclesiastical politics as members of the established kirk when they advocate integration. They are really promoting a "take-over bid". This becomes evident in the embarrassment with which they meet the suggestion that in an integrated system a Roman Catholic might become headmaster of whatever distinguished school you care to mention. Subconsciously at least they think of Catholics as second class citizens and of themselves as an elite which will remain in control.

For a long time most Catholics in Scotland were second class citizens. That is one historical reason for the defence of a special school system cherished by a community too many fo whose members have been faced with the choice of Protestantism or hunger, in the nineteenth century and even more recently. For integration to become a reality there must be a deeper self-criticism on the part of many Scottish Protestants. Unless Catholics are convinced that they will not be discriminated against in an integrated system they cannot be expected to abandon the existing system. Can we be sure that there will be no discrimination on religious grounds? I have a letter written by a recent director of education informing an applicant for a headship in the Strathclyde region that he could not be considered for the post as it was in "a Protestant school". This was perhaps hardly surprising in view of the furore created about the same time by the appointment to a school in Lanarkshire of a janitor who was a Catholic. As in Northern Ireland, there are jobs at stake and not only among the working class.

I can see the possibility of intgration nevertheless, given certain conditions. Again I am thinking of secondary education rather than primary. At secondary level children should be preparing for entry into full citizenship and its responsibilities. Religion still matters in our world and it is important that respect for conscience and an ability to live in mutual respect and toleration should be acquired by everyone as far as possible. This ideal would seem more attainable if we learned to face differences and to live with them, rather than attempting to ignore or evade them as long as possible.

Consequently, I would like to see, in integrated schools, a variety of religion courses which would reflect the actual situation in Scotland and the varied wishes of parents. There would then be a choice open in religion as in science or languages. In Scotland at present this would mean at least three courses in most schools, one representing the Presbyterian tradition, one Catholic and the third Humanist, each taught by the groups they represented. Such a system would stimulate discussion among staff and pupils and encourage the latter to develop adult, personal positions in religion and morals.

Some years ago I drafted proposals for training teachers who would become eligible for posts in the departments of religious studies which I envisaged as part of an integrated system. It was received with every appearance of enthusiasm by those who might have been responsible for its implementation, until Cardinal Gray much to their surprise and dismay accepted the idea. At that point the enthusiasm of my Presbyterian friends suddenly evaporated and only Episcopalians and Humanists showed any further interest.

They illustrated what seems to me an important element in any discussion of integration, the fact that some who give lip-service to the idea rely on the Roman Catholic authorities to block it. They would be seriously disturbed if it came about since it would be a major step towards the disestablishment of religion with consequent loss of privileged positions.

In Scotland today there are two religious establishments set up by Act of Parliament:the Kirk, by an Act of 1929 and the Catholic school system by an Act of 1918. If one system were disestablished it would weaken the position of the others. At present each secures job advantages to numbers of people, often to mediocrity. The kirk has a privileged position in broadcasting, hospital and prison chaplaincies, to take only the more obvious examples. The Catholic school system similarly ensures an employment structure in which competition is reduced.

There are signs of change, made largely through necessity none the less valuable. I have met in a large Catholic school a head of the history department who is an active member of the Salvation Army. In Heriot-Watt University there is an effective team ministry of chaplains. Such instances show what is possible in spite of the strong sectrianism which still exists in some places.

But if we want a more free, pluralist society, with one generally accepted educational system there are awkward facts to be faced more squarely yet and we must tackle the disguised sectarianism which sometimes lurks behind ecumenical gestures. I believe that both the major churches in Scotland should be disestablished; that the fundamental issues of life, the values which shape our society should be discussed in senior schools freely by staff and students alike. Those who profess to believe in freedom of conscience will accept the results "whether they lead to Rome or to Salt Lake City". Those who have faith in the working of the Holy Spirit will not fear the result of living in a more open and therefore more challenging situation than there is at present.

Unemployment and the Scottish economy
symptoms & diagnosis
J.R.Firn

The middle of 1976, a year enshrined for most Scottish economists as the bicentennial of Adam Smith's "Wealth of Nations", is an exceptionally difficult time to discuss the present state of the Scottish economy, and (as ever!) an almost impossible instant to be asked to make predictions about its future. A year earlier, such a task would have seemed much easier. Wages and incomes were steadily rising up towards parity with the U.K. average; the Scottish: U.K. unemployment relative was improving out of all recognition; the Department of Industry's Scottish economic research unit had produced firm evidence that the impact of North Sea oil and gas acitivities was responsible for 40,000 much-needed jobs being created in Scotland; and, for the first time in recent history, Scotland had apparently achieved a small net inward flow of population. While no one would have been foolish enough to believe that all of Scotland's problems were on the way to being solved, these and most of the other oft-quoted economic

51

indicators seemed to show that Scotland was set fair to move into a new era of relative economic prosperity.

A year has passed, and although the long-term economic prognosis for Scotland remains strongly favourable (and incomparably better than one could have hoped for twenty years earlier), it is now possible to detect the first signs of some uncertainty about the ease and the speed with which the Scottish economy can break out of its past low growth pattern. Some of the reasons for this recent caution can be seen by looking in a little more detail at developments of the four major indicators mentioned above. Firstly, official revisions of the annual estimates of migration announced earlier this year have turned a supposed net immigration of population into Scotland over 1973-74 into a net outward flow (albeit an exceptionally small one), and thus the long record of net annual emigration continues. Further, figures for 1974-75 show that the level of net emigration has risen sharply back towards its old level — a development which would have been expected given the long-established relationship between the level of unemployment in Scotland and net emigration.

If there has been a deterioration in Scotland's emigration situation, and after all there are those who would say that Scotland should count herself as being fortunate in having an almost static population, then the same cannot be said of the growth in the employment created by the offshore oil and gas industries — or can it? The estimates of employment associated with North Sea oil and gas have risen substantially since mid-1975, and it is now thought that well over 55,000 people are employed by this sector once allowances are made for multiplier and other indirect effects. But the long-term future of many of these jobs has begun to look less secure than appeared to be the case a year ago, for the relative slowdown in the rate of offshore exploration in Western Europe and more especially the current hiatus in the placing of orders for production platforms has certainly placed a substantial number of these jobs at risk. Indeed, a number of isolated individual communities could find themselves being rapidly transformed into areas of severe economic distress by mid-1977. What is even more certain is that Scotland has already come close to reaching the point of maximum employment creation in the oil and gas sector.

Unemployment in Scotland, traditionally the most important and influential of the major economic indicators, has also begun to deteriorate compared to the U.K. level if the evidence of early 1976 is to be believed. How long such a deterioration will continue is hard to predict from current evidence, but if it continues for much of this coming year — and the current shortage of orders facing many of the firms in the engineering sectors in Scotland suggests it might — then the famed "unemployment relative" may well return to its old relationship, although it would be helped if net emigration were to remain at a high level in 1976. It should also be noted that much of both the long-term improvement and the improvement over the past two years in the unemployment relative has been due not so much to any real improvement in the Scottish unemployment position, but to the relative worsening of the overall U.K. situation.

Whereas three of the indicators have therefore begun to be seen rather differently over the past year, the same cannot be said of the relative improvement of Scottish earnings and wage rates, for these have maintained their rise towards U.K. levels, and indeed in some industries and for some sub-regions of Scotland, earnings stand above those for the U.K. as a whole. The underlying causes of this convergence are still not fully understood: part of it is due to industrial structural factors; part is certainly due to the long tradition of overtime working in the heavy industrial sectors (a little remarked evil); North Sea oil and gas has also had an effect, but the growth of national wage-bargaining has perhaps had the most important impact. What will be interesting over the next few years will be the effect that the recent pay policies have on Scotland's earnings position, but in general terms one can expect that the rate of improvement will slow down in the future. One thing is clear: it is no longer possible to treat Scotland as a low wage area, and this has important implications for policy.

The changes that have taken place in the above, and in other associated economic indicators during the past year, therefore make it difficult to predict the likely future course of the Scottish economy during the immediate future (say to the end of 1977). Obviously much depends on the rate of recovery experienced by the overall U.K. economy, but from the Scottish point of view it is not yet possible to tell whether the events of the past year represent merely a temporary deviation from an otherwise favourable long-term trend, or whether the Scottish economy has reached the latest of its post-war series of crises. The only firm conclusions that can be drawn are that it is dangerous to generalise on the basis of one year's set of figures and that indicators may not be all they're cracked up to be!

In reality no applied economist engaged on a detailed evaluation of Scottish prospects would attempt to monitor the progress of the Scottish economy on the basis of four imperfect aggregate indicators such as those outlined above, and this brings us to one of the most fundamental problems currently facing economists and policy-makers, namely, the sheer difficulty of measuring the performance of the Scottish economy. Many of the more important economic indicators are only made available in a highly aggregated form, and often only after a substantial delay. This latter problem is hard to get around in a society where computer-based reporting systems are distrusted. Those indicators that are published have, at least for Scotland, tended to concentrate on measures relating to employment and unemployment. Very little data emerges on more important aspects such as the value and volume of industrial production; on capital investment; and on productivity. However, this particular complaint should not be laid wholly at the door of the government statistical agencies, for the nature of modern industry has meant that many enterprises, and especially those with a multi-regional nature, no longer keep the kind of records that allow regional measures of production to be produced in a meaningful way. The result is that in the case of production, for example, the Business Statistics Office is forced to employ a range of allocative procedures which are largely responsible for the seeming convergence of productivity (measured in terms of net output-per-man) at the regional level; these problems have also been partly responsible for the fact that an index of industrial production no longer exists for Scotland. It has always struck me as strange that, for example, industrial enterprises receive large amounts of public sector finance under the various industrial and regional development assistance schemes, and yet are allowed to opt out of providing government with the economic and statistical information that is required to monitor the progress and results of such policies. It is akin to giving a patient medicine and not quite knowing whether he's getting better! However, even if such intractable problems could be overcome, and they perhaps could be given a little more determination on the part of the government and a little less obstruction by bodies such as the C.B.I., the most important determinants of the economic progress of a country like Scotland will by their very nature remain unmeasurable. There are problems in defining concepts such as entrepreneurship; or management ability; or technological change, let alone in trying to measure and monitor them. This whole question of economic monitoring provides one of the most exasperating paradoxes in present-day Scotland, for just at the time when economic and political events are producing an increased demand for more information about the changes that are taking place, it is in fact getting harder — at least in key industrial sectors — to collect, process and publish the information that is required to evaluate such change.

This inability to monitor the past and indeed the current performance of the Scottish economy — except in very broad terms — has also had an impact on our understanding of the nature of the problems facing the current generation of policy-makers. Despite a large increase in the number of applied economists interested in Scottish problems (within government, local authorities, industry and the universities) , and despite the development of ever more sophisticated and precise methods of economic analysis, it is clear that only relatively slow progresss has been made towards identifying the real basic problems and constraints that lie behind Scotland's comparatively poor economic performance in the post-war period. But progress there has been, and especially over the last five years, during which time our understanding of the Scottish economy has grown rapidly.

The research that has been undertaken has already had one important outcome, which is now beginning to influence the economic and industrial policies that are being applied for, and within, Scotland. This is the growing conviction that the basic economic problems of Scotland are to be found principally on the supply side, i.e. within Scottish industries and enterprises. Anyone with a knowledge of Scottish economic history, and especially those familiar with, for example, the 1932 Board of Trade **Industrial Survey of the South West of Scotland,** or with the 1946 **Clyde Valley Plan** (which contains a remarkably perceptive chapter on industrial development) , will find the current rediscovery of the supply side emphasis surprising. But there can be little doubt that until relatively recently, Scotland's industrial decline was seen as being the consequence of a steady falling off in international and national **demand** for its products, and government policies were very much orientated towards trying to replace these declining sectors by encouraging the immigration of enterprises active in the new, growth sectors of the national and international economies. No one asked the key question about why it was that Scottish enterprises in the so-called declining sectors failed to forsee the decline and to respond to the threat of it by developing new markets, products and technologies, yet this is precisely the question that must be answered and it remains relevant today. As we shall see below, it is one that is of crucial importance at present in relation to the oil and gas industry.

In fact the roots of the so-called decline of the Scottish indigenous sector (which is essentially an industrial one) probably lie far back in the early years of this century, and therefore, the post-1945 problems are very much seen as the cumulative consequence of decisions taken (or not taken) in earlier periods. Nowhere has the result of the decline of indigenous industrial sector been better seen than in West Central Scotland, which despite its severe economic problems remains the essential powerhouse of the Scottish economy. The hypotheses advanced to explain the root causes of the West Central problem are many and varied: the preference for conspicuous consumption rather than productive investment in the periods of prosperity at the turn of the century (a pointer here perhaps about North Sea oil?); the development of second generation entrepreneurial softness; the slaughter of proto-entrepreneurs on the Somme; and, more recently, the suggestion that the heavy demands made upon Clydeside industry during the First World War may have permanently and irreparably distorted the structure of the local economy. None of these hypotheses have been critically examined, and they offer unlimited opportunities for the new generation of econometric historians to make major contributions to our present understanding of the forces that shape regional change. It must be stressed that such past events are important to our understanding of Scotland's current economic situation: their exclusion by many economists reflects a mistaken belief that the comparative statics of neoclassical economics are more revealing than the long-term dynamics of economic growth.

The recent renewal of interest in the supply-side constraints of Scottish industry has been matched by a growing realisation that the other major problem that confronts Scotland at the present is that of the decline of her major urban areas, not only in the West of Scotland, but also in the Central Region, Tayside and the Lothians. In many ways the economic problems of the old Scottish cities reflect the declining industrial base of inner urban areas, but it is obviously a two-way process. Clydeside remains of course, the ultimate urban problem area in North-West Europe, topping as it does the lists of nearly every undesirable economic, social and cultural indicator. Its older housing is appalling; its industrial base is exceptionally weak; its financial problems are daunting; its political government is hopelessly inept and — dare one say it — partially corrupt; and much of the post-war planning has been characterised by a series of abysmal blunders. Yet, it should be stressed that Clydeside is probably only different from other older urban areas in the U.K. in the degree to which these problems exist. The nature and the causes of urban decline in Scotland are still imperfectly understood, and it is surprising that more research into the economics of urban growth and decline has not been undertaken in Scotland, especially given that most of its population live in or around urban areas.

The case of Glasgow illustrates the need for more work to be done in this area. Ever since the Clyde Valley Plan of 1946, there has been a continuous policy of encouraging industry and population to move out of Glasgow to relocate in the new towns and around the periphery of the city. From a housing conditions viewpoint, this approach had much to recommend it, but it has consistently neglected the needs of urban industry with the present dire consequences. Urban industry is admittedly exceptionally difficult to understand, but we do know that manufacturing and service sector enterprises in a city like Glasgow are part of a highly integrated organic complex of trades and professions which have developed over a long period of time. Although much of the industrial decline of inner Glasgow has probably been due to industrial rather than locational factors, the physical planning policies adopted in the post-war period have persistently failed to understand the nature of the urban economy and especially the needs of manufacturing industry. Indeed, in some of the earlier redevelopment areas, industry was treated very much as a planning residual. The regeneration of industry in the inner areas of Glasgow will therefore be an important area of policy in the future, but there are fears that the decline of the inner city economy may already have got out of hand. Population continues to pour out of the city, and some of the more recent population projections for the 1980s are ominous indeed. In fact, most of Scotland's annual net migration of population has its base in the Strathclyde Region. Other urban areas in Scotland have their economic and social problems, but all are dwarfed by the scale of the Clydeside problem. However, what is required is not to stand around wringing one's hands in despair, but to accept the urban problem as an exciting and difficult challenge.

The industrial and urban problems of Scotland are but two of the many constraints to Scottish economic growth that must be overcome in the future, if this country is to achieve its undoubted potential. There are many other areas of the country's social and economic structure where severe problems exist. They require to be examined at greater length than is possible in a brief survey such as this, but prime candidates for more detailed policy-orientated analysis must include amongst others, industrial relations, the balance and sources of public sector expenditure, and especially, the crucial topic of housing. Perhaps the final word that should be said about the problems existing in the Scottish economy, is that we are now fairly certain that we have identified the broad areas of concern, but that we have still a long way to go before we can be sure that we really understand the causal mechanisms and relationships that produce the problems. Until we are much further along in this latter stage, it will be difficult to know whether in fact the issues that concern us will be amenable to policy implemented within Scotland.

If it is hard to identify the real constraints that exist within Scottish industry, or within urban economies, it is also exceptionally difficult to isolate the real, cast-iron areas of economic potential that exist. Yet the identification of potential economic growth sectors is important if one wishes to take some role in steering an economy such as Scotland's. Certainly Scotland has a superb natural resource base, and one which is probably well suited to the requirements of the coming century. It has also an exceptionally well-endowed labour force, even though it has not been wisely utilised, and a pool of entrepreneurial talent that future economic policies must, as a priority, aim to make more active. It has, despite the long history of economic and industrial decline, a substantial number of commercial and manufacturing enterprises in both the public and private sectors that are both dynamic and profitable, and which therefore deserve greater encouragement. Unfortunately, as we shall see below, rather too much attention has been devoted to intervening in a negative fashion, but there can be little doubt that a fundamental reappraisal of industrial and regional policy objectives will be forthcoming.

However, there are those who feel that any discussion about the identification of economic potential must be littered with examples of actual individual sectors that are growth candidates. Unfortunately, the literature of development economics in both the developed and the third world is replete with unfortunate experiences of particular industries or products or commodities being labelled as growth sectors, and then turning sour. Therefore, to those who would offer fish farming, or armaments manufacture, or pollution control devices, or vehicles — to name only some of those industries advanced as being suitable for Scotland during the last year — I would remind them that only a decade ago, the electronics industry was seen as the sector with a golden future in Scotland. The labour-shedding that has taken place in this particular industry during the present recession has put some of the older "declining" industries to shame, and the international economics of the major multinational companies involved in the sector would not seem to hold out a prosperous long-term future for many of the plants now operating in Scotland. Most of the new areas of real potential are, by virtue of their very nature, hard to predict, and one would expect such "potential" to reveal itself as the economy develops. There are policy initiatives that can be introduced to help identify, develop, and often create growth products and sectors, and principal among such policies are measures intended to increase the amount of applied research and development undertaken in a country, thereby raising the level of that particular country's technology. Once again, however, the past experience of other countries that have chosen to pursue this particular route to international competitiveness does not altogether encourage us to believe that it is an infallible method of creating potential. If Scotland can become a healthy, growing and competitive economy, then its companies and industries will provide the potential automatically.

Policies designed to encourage or direct technological change have always proved to be elusive, but fortunately we can be much surer about policy requirements in more general terms when discussing the Scottish economy. There are however two preliminary points that must be made: both have been made before, but both can bear repeating. Firstly, the very open nature of the Scottish economy due to its particular industrial mix (both in product and organisational terms) means that it is firmly linked into both the United Kingdom and world economies. Because of this there are distinct limits to the effectiveness of economic and industrial policies designed to operate in Scotland alone, and until the Scottish economy develops a greater measure of self-reliance (easy to say, but desperately difficult to achieve) it is always liable to be blown off any policy course by the pressure of external events. Secondly, we can be sure that no matter what policies are developed and employed, the ultimate objectives in terms of achieving a radical restructuring of the Scottish commercial and industrial base will not be achieved easily, nor with any great speed: unfortunately, economic development is neither sudden nor spectacular.

There is only space in this article to discuss very briefly the three policy areas that I consider to be the most important in the immediate future: the need to restructure industry; the urgent case for adopting a national urban development strategy; and the rather special case of oil and gas.

Perhaps the most fundamental requirement in the industrial policy debate that is now beginning to take place in Scotland is the realisation that it **is** an industrial policy that is required, and not merely some variant of existing regional policies. In retrospect, the economic rationale behind the application of U.K. regional policy to Scotland, and indeed to other lagging regions of the U.K., has been pretty minimal. The focus of past effort has been essentially on improving the demand for labour in Scotland by encouraging the inter-regional and inter-national mobility of enterprises, and the central objective of the approach has been to reduce unemployment by any means possible. This will in future be seen as one of the curses of twentieth century Scottish economic policy-making, primarily because it has resulted in a whole series of measures aimed at treating the **symptoms** of industrial decline, rather than tackling the underlying forces, constraints and factor rigidities that have been responsible for the decline. Perhaps this is being rather harsh on those involved in developing the policies, for it is only recently, with the benefit of hindsight, that we have come to see that a continuation of past policies is likely to prove disastrous. There are two reasons.

Firstly, the old golden days of mobile industry within the U.K. being used as the spearhead of regional policy are gone. Areas such as the South-East and the West Midlands, where the recent recession pushed up unemployment rates to "development area" levels, are now becoming increasingly resentful about much of their industrial growth being sent to other areas of the U.K. Their demands to retain such new industry as is created are   likely to become ever louder , and are almost certain   to figure strongly in the economic component of any English backlash on the devolution issue. Secondly, manufacturing industry is becoming more capital intensive, and thus there will be fewer new manufacturing jobs made available for distribution to the regions by any future regional policy. Further, the competition for these jobs is likely to be fierce. The only sensible way of proceeding in such a situation is to develop a much greater industrial component in Scottish development policies, and specifically, these must aim at attacking the major industrial constraints, which as we have seen above, lie overwhelmingly on the supply side. The types of action that are required are perhaps too complex and technical to be discussed here, but they must include measures to improve the prospects for entrepreneurs; they must aim at supporting industrial success rather than failure; and must accept that Scotland has become a mixed economy that is firmly and irretrievably integrated with the rest of the U.K. In general terms, the best way of achieving a measure of success with such industrial policies would seem to lie in adopting what economists term a micro-orientated approach to industrial strategy, but this, as noted above, requires better information on the detailed changes that are taking place within companies. It also requires a much closer relationship between government and companies; this does not mean however greater government intervention in the old-fashioned sense of the word, but rather a much more detailed understanding of what is going on. One major immediate priority must be the inclusion of a Scottish component in the national (U.K.) industrial strategy that is currently being evolved by the central government.

On the urban side, the prospects for a major initiative to solve the deep-rooted problems of the older inner areas of Scottish cities have improved immeasurably. The recent long overdue cancellation of plans to develop Stonehouse into a New Town is perhaps the first step towards a reconcentration of resources towards the needs of the existing cities, and the decision by the Scottish Office to launch a massive £140 mn. redevelopment programme in Glasgow's East End offers the chance for a real breakthrough in trying to revivify the economy of Scotland's most important industrial area. However, for such an urban redevelopment programme to succeed, a number of prior conditions are obviously necessary. Firstly, there must be some agreement about the goals and objectives of the overall programme, and a much greater determination to state the objectives with more precision. If goals are only vaguely specified, then no matter how laudable the intentions behind the programme, and no matter how committed the administrators involved in implementing the policy, it will still be difficult to measure the achievement of objectives. In the past, political pressures have often prevented goals being specified, because non-achievement can mean political ruin. In the future we must get round this particular self-destructive approach, and try to achieve a greater degree of consensus on objectives so that long-term programmes in areas like urban development are not being constantly revised for political motives alone. Secondly, an urban programme — especially one centred on Clydeside — does require to have a substantial amount of Scotland's total resources being injected into it, not merely for physical planning ends such as housing, but also for programmes designed to stimulate industry of the type outlined above. A major urban development programme could, after all, provide an important stimulus to industrial growth in its own right, if a conscious policy was adopted of maximising local involvement. But to have any chance of success, experience in development economics indicates that such a programme must have a relatively big impact over a relatively short space of time, and this can only be achieved if a conscious decision is made to shift a substantial amount of Scotland's resources into this area. This in turn requires a review of our public expenditure programmes (especially now that the Layfield Report on Local Government Finance has been published) and this is in practice unlikely until the Scottish Assembly has been established. What can be predicted is that an urban development programme of this type could become Scotland's dominant domestic policy concern throughout the last part of this century.

Finally, what about the complex question of oil and gas, and its impact on the Scottish economy? Many of the variables involved here are overtly political by nature, and thus I would not want to introduce them here. Certainly, as was noted above, the direct impact in terms of job creation may already have reached its maximum. For the level to rise further would imply almost unbelievably optimistic estimates of future exploration and production activity; of platform ordering; and of the export prospects for Scottish-made offshore equipment. In fact, an economist reviewing the Scottish economy in 2000 A.D. (which is closer to us than the Second World War!) may conclude that the way the oil and gas issue has been handled in Scotland offers a perfect example of how **not** to do things. It is already clear that some fundamental mistakes — some of which **were** predictable — have been made, and of these the most glaring concerns the policy towards production platform sites. Even in the most optimistic days of exploration activity there were those who warned of the dangers of having too many sites designated; of possible future shortages of orders; of the problems involved in ignoring technological change; and of the permanent damage that might well be done to isolated communities suddenly faced with a large-scale influx of employment of an inherently temporary nature. Events have proved that these cynics were right, and that many of the "experts" trotted forward by the government departments involved were wrong. The events at Kishorn have, for example, shown that "economic necessity" can run rings round, over and through planning conditions unless very tight control is exercised; and I would be personally very surprised if the Committee of Public Accounts did not investigate the complete waste of public funds involved in the Portvadie and Hunterston platform sites. There is anyway now growing agreement that large offshore platforms may turn out to be something of a temporary phenomenon, as the speed of technological change in offshore engineering is exceptionally high.

Unfortunately, all the evidence seems to show that Scottish companies, with a few notable exceptions, have not contributed much to developing new and original offshore technologies, and thus there is now a distinct possibility that the oil and gas industry will have passed industrial Scotland by. I would also suggest that hopes of the large-scale exporting of Scottish-made offshore products to other oil and gas provinces, especially those in the third world, may prove to be slightly misplaced, in that many of the countries that are moving into offshore exploration, such as India and China, have well-developed engineering industries that are keen to break into these new areas, and governments that place importance on import-substitution as a means of conserving scarce foreign-exchange. In such conditions joint ventures or licensing becomes important, and this normally requires the possession of the relevant technology, or at the very least exceptionally good financing facilities and terms. Thus, we have to look towards Scottish involvement in the oil and gas revenues as being the way in which the major economic impact will come, and this is essentially a political question; or towards greater Scottish involvement in the downstream processing activities, and this is one area where I think we should look for more state participation via the Scottish Development Agency or the British National Oil Corporation

In conclusion, it can be said that the recent development of some reservations about the underlying strength of Scotland's economic position does not in any way mean that there is cause for alarm, and it certainly should not force us into taking an alternative and more pessimistic view of future prospects. Indeed, the development of some caution is to be encouraged if it results in a more realistic attitude being taken towards both the problems and potential of the Scottish economy, and if it raises the standard of debate about the types of policies that will be required to achieve the fundamental restructuring of the Scottish economy that most observers agree is necessary.

Reactions to the Devolution White Paper

J.G.Kellas

When the White Paper on Devolution was published on 27 November 1975, it immediately raised a storm of controversy in Scotland and beyond. For it appeared that while 'Home Rule for Scotland and Wales' was at last practical politics and was to be implemented by the Labour Government, the nature of that Home Rule was far from satisfactory to opinion in Scotland, or in England.

To the majority of Scots, it seemed that it 'did not go far enough'. To most in England, on the other hand, it represented a 'threat to the unity of the United Kingdom', or the first step on the 'slippery slope' to Scottish independence.

The sort of devolution (the new name for Home Rule) proposed by the Government was supposed to provide for 'a massive handover to the new elected Assemblies of responsibility for the domestic affairs of Scotland and Wales, within the firm continuing frame work of the United Kingdom' (par. 4). In a phrase the government revealed that high hopes and strong fears were invoked by its scheme.

The 'massive handover' concerned the more local functions of central government, such as education, housing, health, roads and transport, and environmental planning. These are all at present under the control of the Scottish Office in Edinburgh, and would now come under the Scottish Assembly. But the 'firm continuing framework of the United Kingdom' meant that major functions of central government such as taxation, economic management and industrial development remained with the UK

Government, either in the Scottish Office, or in other Whitehall departments. Moreover, the 'sovereignty of Parliament' over all the affairs of the country was to be maintained intact, and new powers of 'veto' were introduced: a veto over **ultra vires** Bills of the Scottish Assembly, and a 'policy' veto over Scottish Assembly Bills which were 'unacceptable on policy grounds' to the UK Government. The first veto would be exercised solely by the Secretary of State   for Scotland, and the second by the Secretary of State with the confirmation of Parliament (pars. 56-60).

It was explained that any surrender of the UK Government and Parliament's sovereignty 'would imply federalism, not devolution', and it was added for emphasis later on that those who were demanding a share of the oil revenues for a Scottish government were 'in effect demanding a separate Scottish state. The circle cannot be squared: it is not possible for Scotland - or any other part of the United Kingdom - to enjoy rights which can only go with separatism yet not have separatism itself' (par. 97).

Thus two alternatives to devolution, federalism and 'separatism', were firmly ruled out, on the rather shaky grounds that the sovereignty of Parliament and the monopoly of oil revenues by the central government were principles that could not be negotiated.

This left a kind of Home Rule eminently suitable as an extension of the local government system, but not one which could meet the discontents associated with the rise in nationalism, and the feeling that economic and social deprivation in Scotland could be tackled through the application of oil revenues to the regeneration of the Scottish economy. Yet such seemed to be the situation in Scotland: the Scottish National Party had risen to 30 per cent of the vote and 11 MPs in October 1974. The focus of the political debate in Scotland was on the run-down nature of the economy and its potential salvation through the discoveries of North Sea oil.

This was not of course how devolution or Scottish problems were viewed in London, or in the depressed regions of England. In London, the argument ran that Scotland was receiving more per head in public expenditure than other parts of the country, and had been given special attention in regional incentives to attract industry. It had no right to pre-empt itself a further bonus from oil revenues, these were   in any case mortgaged for the elimination of the British balance of payments deficit. While Scotland might be entitled to a further strengthening of its existing governmental structure, it could not hope to transform its function into those of major policy-making in economic and social affairs. If the 'political and economic unity' of the United Kingdom were to be preserved, these must remain in London.

In the regions of England, the threat that Scotland might gain added political leverage through devolution, and so win a larger slice of the national cake, made many English M.P.s anxious to resist a Scottish Assembly. Some used the argument that their own regions were equally entitled to devolution; others accepted that few English people desired a parallel set of institutions in the English regions to those proposed for Scotland, yet they too opposed the Scottish proposals. In either case, Scotland should not get its Assembly, for that meant shifting resources

63

away from their constituencies.

Clearly, the resolution of the devolution issue in British politics depends on the balance between Scottish aspirations and English fears. How far would the Scots really go towards independence, and how far would the English go in resisting 'meaningful' or 'maximalist' devolution (that is, devolution with economic powers, and with freedom from the vetoes of London)?

Put in this way, the problem exaggerates the degree of Scottish-English antagonism, even if it is essentially accurate. Within Scotland, there are several strands of opinion on the constitutional issue, ranging from the supporters of the status quo, to the 'separatists' (a word shunned by the Nationalists). These strands cut across party lines, and across economic interests, social and educational sectors, and the media. There is no easy formula to say who is where on the Home Rule issue in Scotland. Within each political party there are pro- and anti-devolution wings, although the Liberals and SNP leaders   are much more united than the Labour and Conservative ones. Liberal and SNP supporters, however, display the same diversity of opinion as do Labour and Conservative supporters. For example, it is possible to find crypto-nationalists in the Conservative and Labour parties who would like a strong Scottish government with control over oil revenues. And there are many SNP voters who have no interest in the question of Scottish self government at all. They could be called 'protest' or 'tactical' voters, depending on their motivations.

In England, there are some who are passionate about the 'unity of Britain' and the 'sovereignty of Parliament', and who consider that Scottish home rule aspirations are dangerous. But the majority are probably uninterested in constitutional matters, and, since the EEC Referendum of June 1975, have stopped arguing about sovereignty and national unity. They are especially uninterested in and uninformed about Scottish questions, and would be most surprised to learn of the separate Scottish legal, educational, administrative, and local government systems. While they are annoyed to find that Britain is not as homogeneous and as united as they think it is, they are ultimately unconcerned about such diversity, as long as it does not interfere with their own lives.

To finding a solution to the devolution question in Scotland, any British government must take account of the variety of opinion which is expressed on the matter. This opinion takes various forms, notably popular feelings in elections and surveys, and elite opinion in the House of Commons, the main interest groups, and in the media. In each case, there is an English and a Scottish form to that opinion.

It is obvious that electoral considerations and not elite opinion have provided the driving force in the devolution issue. Without the dramatic rise in the votes for SNP, there would have been no White Paper in 1975. Much of the debate in the other parties has concerned the need to win back votes from the SNP, and generally to satisfy Scottish opinion on home rule.

In Scotland, this has of course most concerned the M.P.s themselves, whose very seats are in danger. But in England, the party managers, have also been determined that their support in Scotland should not wither away, thereby making the formation of a government difficult. Labour, with 41 out of the 71 seats in Scotland , needs the Scottish contingent if it is to form a Government. The Conservatives, with only 16 M.P.s in Scotland, are less dependent on the Scottish seats, though they look back nostalgically to 1955 when the Party had 36 seats in Scotland. Some believe that a home rule platform might regain some of their seats.

The distinction between M.P.s and party managers in England explains some of the differences in their reactions to devolution. To the managers, and party leaders, devolution is a means of winning seats in Scotland. To the English M.P.s, there is no threat to their seats from Scotland, and their constituency interests are not favourable (for reasons already given) to Scottish devolution. Thus the party leaders in the House of Commons find it difficult to bring their English colleagues into line in support of devolution.

The threat to major party seats in Scotland remained evident after the publication of the White Paper. Opinion polls gave adverse results on its acceptibility, and local elections showed a strong advance for the SNP. In general, the SNP surged forward in public support from November 1975 to January 1976, thereafter falling back to its October 1974 level of 30 per cent support. There was, however, no parliamentary by-election in the period.

Among the political elite in Scotland, there was considerable agitation. Two M.P.s, Jim Sillars and John Robertson, actually deserted the Labour Party in December 1975, to form their own 'Scottish Labour Party'. One aim of this party was to secure the maximum amount of devolution or independence compatible with membership of the United Kingdom. Such devolution would include separate Scottish representation at the European Community, and strong economic powers for a Scottish Government.

In response, the Labour Party in Scotland expelled the secessionists, although the Labour Whips in the House of Commons continued to count them in the Labour total. It also decided to strengthen the White Paper proposals, by transferring the Scottish Development Agency to the Scottish Assembly, and by removing the veto powers from the UK Government, leaving only the over riding power of an Act of the UK Parliament. All this was passed at the Scottish conference in March 1976, and seemed to be accepted by the Labour Government. The anti-devolution faction within the Labour Party in Scotland, very strong before 1974, and formerly including the Labour Secretary of State for Scotland, William Ross (1964-70, 1974-76), made some ground at the 1976 conference, but the devolution programme was now practically unanimously carried. It was strongly supported by the principal trade unions, such as the Mineworkers, Transport and General Workers, and Engineering Workers. The leading anti-devolutionists were Tam Dalyell M.P. and Willie Hamilton, M.P..

At the start of 1976, the Labour Party in Scotland launched a campaign, 'Devolution **not** Separation', but this seemed to fizzle out quite quickly. It was evident that Labour found it difficult to argue against nationalism in Scotland, while itself being accused of nationalism by anti-devolutionists, in Scotland and in England. The absence of enthusiasm for devolution among English Labour M.P.s made the campaign rather unrealistic as an

65

expression of Labour belief.

The Conservative Party was also faced with disunion in its ranks, within Scotland and between Scotland and England. The Scottish Conservative Party had first decided to support a Scottish Assembly in 1968, and had re-affirmed that view in 1970, 1974, and 1975. (but not 1973). This policy was more the result of decisions at the top of the party, than of grass-roots demand, and by May 1976 the grass-roots anti-devolutionists had formed themselves into a faction, the 'Keep Britain United' campaign. The leaders were Iain Sproat , M.P., Teddy Taylor, M.P. and Michael Clark Hutchison, M.P. These anti-devolutionists made a much bigger showing at the Scottish Conservative Conference in 1976 than their couterparts in the Scottish Labour Conference. They challenged their leaders' proposals for a Scottish Assembly, and were able to muster over a third of the delegates, despite the presence at the conference of leaders such as Margaret Thatcher, William Whitelaw, and Lord Home, all of whom supported a Scottish Assembly.

Behind this disunity in Scotland, there was the same difference between the Scottish and English M.P.s. Only five of the sixteen Scottish Conservative M.P.s were hostile to devolution, but a meeting of Conservative back benchers in the House of Commons just before the Scottish conference showed a large anti-devolution group from English constituencics.

The Conservative leadership was able to resolve this problem, at least temporarily. Even before the White Paper came out, the Conservatives showed their opposition to the Labour plans, for they wanted to see the establishment of a Scottish Assembly **without** a Scottish Executive. There would thus be two legislative bodies (Edinburgh and Westminster), but only one Government (UK Government in London).

The plan was to take 2nd Readings and Committee and Report stages of Scottish Bills in Edinburgh. Thus, a directly elected Scottish Assembly could control Scottish legislation. Or could it? It was not at all clear whether the Tories were overlooking - or counting on others to overlook - the possibility that Bills thus produced could still, in principle, be rejected at final Reading stage, or during House of Lords proceedings at Westminster.

While this was obviously not enough to silence the anti-devolutionists in the party, in practical terms it meant that the Conservatives would be opposed to the Labour Bill, and would thus be united against any devolution on offer in the immediate future. Were they to beretumed to power, however, they would be faced with implementing their own scheme, over the opposition of many of their supporters, and presumably over the opposition of public opinion in Scotland, which favoured at the very least the Labour proposals.

The Liberal Party was going through a bad patch in late 1975 to mid 1976. Its electoral support had declined badly in England, and was no healthier in Scotland, were it had reached a mere eight per cent in 1974. In May 1976 it lost its leader, Jeremy Thorpe. Although its federal solution was the one most favoured by the Scottish people, if opinion polls are to be believed, it could not sell this electorally in the absence of the emotional appeal of nationalism, and the superior organisation of the SNP. Moreover, it had only three M.P.s from Scotland to make its case, compared to the eleven SNP M.P.s.

As with the Labour and Conservative Parties, there was a division between the Scottish and English sections of the Liberal Party. The Scottish Liberal Party wanted a fully-fledged federal system based on Scotland, England, Wales and Northern Ireland. The Liberal Party in England, did not wish to see an English Parliament set up, and supported instead several English regional parliaments. The Scottish Liberals asserted that 50 per cent of the revenues from North Sea Oil should accrue to a Scottish government. The (English) Liberal Party did not make such a claim. While Jo Grimmond (M.P. for Orkney and Shetland) became leader in May 1976, he was not in a very strong position to re-unite the Party on devolution, for his own Shetland constituents had expressed through their local council their opposition to Scottish devolution. The reasons for this relate to the very successful financial deal that Shetland had made with the oil companies, and the special powers granted by Act of Parliament to Shetland Island Council. There were fears that a Scottish government would revoke some of these privileges in the interests of the more populated areas of Scotland, which were suffering from economic decline.

The Scottish National Party, as the party of national independence, did not support the White Paper, which it saw as not going nearly far enough. It proposed an amendment in the House of Commons to the motion to 'Take Note' of the White Paper, regretting that the Assemblies were to be given no meaningful control over their economies (19 January 1976). This received 27 votes (12 Nationalists, 12 Liberals, 2 'Scottish Labour Party') and one Labour (David Lambie, M.P. for Central Ayrshire) . But when the Conservatives put down **their** motion condemning the White Paper, the SNP rallied to its support, and the general SNP view was that ' half a loaf' was better than no bread. With only 20 per cent of the Scottish electorate in favour of Scottish independence according to surveys, the SNP was careful to avoid appearing to wish to wreck devolution in order to produce independence Indeed, Donald Stewart, M.P., the leader of the SNP in Parliament, went so far as to say that they had no intention of seeking the 'Break-up of the United Kingdom'. Thus the SNP was somewhat afraid that if it pressed its case too far there might be a backlash against it in **Scotland** as well as in England, and that devolution might fail to be realised. While this might conceivably hasten independence, it might also mean the perpetuation of the status quo.

The Communist Party, while electorally insignificant, spoke strongly through individual members in prominent positions in the trade union movement. The Party wanted a 'Maximalist'' system of devolution with a share of oil revenues, more on the lines of a federal system. Jimmy Reid of the Engineers and and U.C.S. 'work-in', Jimmy Milne, General Secretary of the STUC, and Mick McGahey of the Scottish Mineworkers, were Communists who pressed for economic powers to be given to the Scottish Assembly.

Outside the political parties, the interests of Scotland voiced their opinions. Some of these interests were closely allied to the parties themselves. The individual trade unions have already been mentioned in the context of the Labour Party Scottish Conference. The Scottish Trades Union Congress has taken a 'maximalist' position on devolution for some years, and in 1976 re-affirmed its desire to see further economic powers devolved to Scotland. But it did not press this strongly after the Labour Party in Scotland strengthened its proposals in March 1976. It then preferred to fall into line with 'official' Labour thinking. Labour Parties in local government, too, moved from an anti-devolution stance in 1974 to one supporting the White Paper proposals. Fears were frequently expressed, however, that the local government structure as reorganised in 1974 on a 'regional' and 'district' basis might prove to be vulnerable, in the event of devolution. Most regional authorities sought to prevent the Scottish Assembly acting to abolish the regions in the near future; district authorities tended to look to a one-tier system of local government under devolution, in which the one tier would be the district.

The interests most closely associated with the Conservative Party are the business organisations, the farmers, landowners, and some professional bodies such as the British Medical Association. None of these, however, occupies a position in the Conservative Party similar to that of the trade union movement within the structure of the Labour Party. Thus, their influence on Conservative policy making is somewhat less. The CBI, the Chambers of Commerce, and the farmers were careful not to attack the principle of devolution as such, but were clearly opposed to the Labour proposals. Conservative held local authorities, such as Grampian and Tayside Regions, also opposed Devolution.

Despite their large measure of professional devolution in Scottish organisations, the Scottish judges, university principals and lecturers, and doctors were not in favour of being brought under the control of a Scottish Assembly. The White Paper had carefully excluded the courts, universities, and pay and conditions in the health service, from the Scottish Assembly's powers. Nevertheless, it provisionally favoured the devolution of power to legislate about the control of the legal, teaching, health and town planning professions (but not architects and engineers). It was perhaps this aspect that worried the judges and doctors most.

One business promotion body that clearly favoured devolution was the Scottish Council (Development and Industry). This body, made up of representatives of industry, trade unions, local government, and central government, had long pressed for 'decentralisation' of political and economic power to Scotland. It was anxious to secure a form of devolution which would include the power to shape the Scottish economy through taxation powers and special regional incentives. It also desired the decentralisation of decision making within industry itself. The Scottish Council Research Institute reported before the White Paper came out that half of the revenues from North Sea oil should be given to a Scottish Government.

Some prominent businessmen in Scotland moved to a devolutionist or nationalist stance. Sir William McEwan Younger, chairman of the Scottish Conservatives from 1971 to 1974, took an intense dislike to 'Whitehall over centralisation' in the early 1970s, and warned the Scottish Conservative conference in May 1976 that if devolution were blocked at Westminster, he would be tempted to vote for independence. Sir Hugh Fraser, the commercial magnate, had already announced his conversion to the SNP in 1974.

Other fears were expressed that standards or prestige would decline in a devolved system of education, health and judicial administration. University teachers were predominantly in favour of retaining the links with the University Grants Committee, the research councils, and the Department of Education and Science. There was, however, a growing faction within the Association of University Teachers (Scotland) that wished to unify the Scottish educational system under devolution. The National Union of Students in Scotland supported this. At the same time, the Scottish Secondary Teachers Association considered that devolution would be a waste of time for Scottish schools, since the Westminster M.P.s would leave control over Scottish education in London. The judges of the Court of Session pronounced collectively against devolution of the Court; Lord Wheatley, speaking on their behalf in the House of Lords on 27 January 1976, stressed the 'derogation of the status' of the Scottish courts if they were to be removed from the responsibility of the 'Sovereign Parliament' at Westminster. The Scottish Bar, represented by the Faculty of Advocates, and the solicitors, represented by the Law Society of Scotland, appeared to favour devolution. Both these bodies were more inclined to free Scots Law from the constraints imposed on it by Westminster procedures and politics, and looked towards a much more independent and purely Scottish legal system. Lord Hunter, Chairman of the Scottish Law Commission, made several speeches in 1975 and 1976, voicing similar sentiments. In particular, Scots lawyers called for a single legal department of Scottish government which would speak for Scots Law, not only in Britain but also in the European Community.

A most significant reaction to the White Paper came from the newspapers and broadcasting in Scotland. Bridging the gap between 'mass' and 'elite' opinion, the media reflected as well as shaped the aspirations of the people of Scotland. The 'quality' newspapers, **The Scotsman,** and **Glasgow Herald,** take the place among middle class readers in Scotland occupied by the **Daily Telegraph** the **Times,** and the **Guardian** in England. The **Scotsman** greeted the publication of the White Paper with the headline 'Instant fury on plan for an Assembly in chains' (28 November 1975). It was in no doubt that only a federal solution was appropriate for Scotland. The **Glasgow Herald** (owned by Sir Hugh Fraser, now an SNP supporter) had previously opposed devolution, but now supported the White Paper as 'the first step towards realistic devolution'. Its front page headline, however, ran 'Charter for Conflict: Government attacked on all sides'. The English 'quality' press, on the other hand, was distinctly cool, and the **Daily Telegraph** said that 'there is no subject that is less relevant to the real problems facing the people of Britain than this'. The **Times** grudgingly acknowledged that devolution 'is not an exercise in pursuit of the ideal; it is a recognition of necessity', and the **Financial Times** warned against 'A surplus of government', but supported devolution in principle. The **Guardian** gave a 'qualified, apprehensive welcome' under the headline 'On the edge of the slope looking over'. The **Sunday Times** and **Observer** shared this caution (30 November 1975).

The popular press in Scotland is also distinct from that in England. Even the **Daily Express** comes out in a separate edition, the **Scottish Daily Express,** with separate editorials. The Scottish editor wrote that the White Paper was 'a black betrayal of the people of Scotland who aspired to a greater say in the running of their own affairs. It makes a sham of the Scottish Assembly'. The **Daily Record** headlined 'We were PROMISED, more, now . . . WE WANT MORE because, Harold, your deal is just not good enough'. But its sister IPC paper in England, the **Daily Mirror,** wrote 'It's the least that could be offered and also the most'. The London **Daily Mail** said 'Great Brtain needs devolution like it needs a hole in the head', and the **News of the World** called devolution 'apartheid'. But the Glasgow **Sunday Mail** pronounced ominously, ' that if devolution were stopped because of the English backlash then next time they'll find Scots all speaking with one voice. And the word that voice will be using will be something a damn sight more extreme than Devolution'. The **Press and Journal** (Aberdeen) and the D. C. Thomson press (Dundee) was non-committal, tending to opposition. Most other Scottish papers supported devolution, and only the **Scottish Daily News** (emergency edition) declared 'It must be independence or nothing at all. There's no halfway house'.

While the broadcaster in Scotland could not give an opinion on the white Paper, he certainly gave devolution ample time on TV and radio. Both the BBC and STV discussed the subject for weeks on end, with interest dying around February 1976. But even then, the subject picked up once more with the round of Scottish party conferences from March to May.

All this exposure for devolution in the media gave the impression that the issue was one of the highest priority for the Scottish electorate. Yet surveys continued to show that few in fact placed it on a par with inflation, unemployment and other socio-economic issues. The paradox could only be resolved if one interpreted the 'ends' of policy as dependent on the means (in this case, devolution). The Scottish people might still show the ends as priorities but look towards constitutional change for their realisation.

Since the publication of the White Paper in November 1975, Scottish politics have remained fairly static. No parliamentary advances have been made by the SNP, in the absence of by-elections. Only minor changes have been made in party policies, though some of these (e.g. the Labour policy on the White Paper) have been strongly argued over. The new Scottish Labour Party, after an initial splash, has not yet produced a wave of support. Perhaps more movement has occurred in England, which is

70

'Wakening up' to devolution.

The problem of finding a solution to the government of Scotland will continue to dominate British politics for many years to come. Even if Scottish nationalism declines electorally, the experience of the last few years has put the question of devolution firmly on the agenda. Far too many parties, organisations and individuals are now committed to it to allow it to drop, although there may well be a temporary setback in the House of Commons (or House of Lords).

More importantly, the changing structure of Scottish society and its economy puts Scotland at the forefront on European politics in the late 1970s and 1980s. The focus on North Sea Oil, the new political generation in Scotland, and the changing nature of the party system almost guarantees to Scotland a new power within Britain and the European Community. After 270 years of 'incorporating union' with England, Scotland still retains a strong British identity and sympathy. But the balance of union is being altered in the direction of the statehood which was ended in 1707, just as Britain itself is moving hesitatingly towards the European Community, after having been 'outside Europe' for five hundred years. These grand changes of politics are only dimly perceived in the Scotland of 1976.

We reprint here the full text of Lord Wheatley's speech in the House of Lords of January 27 in which he gave the views of the judges of the Court of Session "Our Changing Democracy"(1). Their views on the role of the judiciary in a Scotland partly governed by the Assembly received much comment. Professor MacCormick's comment, published in **The Scotsman**, was amongst the most notable. Professor MacCormick has expanded his earlier statement for the **Yearbook.**

Accountability Professionalism & The Scottish Judiciary

Lord Wheatley D.N.MacCormick

Lord Wheatley

My Lords, I am afraid that I intend to depart from the pattern which the debate has so far taken and that for what I conceive to be a very good reason. The judges of the High Court in Scotland were invited to give their observations on the White Paper with particular reference to those matters in which they had a particular professional interest. These included matters such as the court system and its administration and where responsibility for that should lie. We accepted that invitation and came to a

1. **Our Changing Democracy: Devolution to Scotland and Wales** (1975 Cmnd. 6348), hereinafter referred to as "The White Paper".

collective judgment and the views which I shall express here this evening are the unanimous views of all the High Court judges in Scotland. I appreciate that normally a Member of your Lordships' House is expected to present his own views rather than to be the representative of those of others but, in these peculiar circumstances, the fact that the views which I am expressing represent the unanimous views of the judges of the High Court of Scotland will carry much more weight than could any personal contribution of my own. However, that very considerably circumscribes the area which I can cover.

Secondly, there is, as your Lordships know, a convention which we in Scotland accept. It is that judges should not become involved in public political controversy. As I know from personal experience on several occasions when a judge has been a member of a Royal Commission or of a departmental Committee of Inquiry, it is not only reasonable but probably right that he should explain publicly the recommendations of the Commission or committee and the reasons for them. However, when the subject enters the political arena and becomes politically controversial, we assume an elective silence on the political issues and confine ourselves, if we intervene at all, to constitutional or legal questions or views on practical matters affecting the law and its administration, where our views may naturally be expected and sought.

So, when the Scottish High Court judges considered the proposals in the White Paper in the narrow fields to which their attention had been directed, they did not consider those aspects with a political connotation or involvement. However, we sought to collect the views of all the judges on other matters. What we did not attempt to obtain, even had it been possible — which I doubt — were the collective views of the judges on whether or not there should be an Assembly and, if there were, what form it should take and what powers it should have. We confined ourselves to such matters as the law and the system of the courts and their administration on which we felt we were qualified to speak. We also considered the question of **vires**, to which reference has already been made by a number of noble Lords. Our views in that situation were naturally based on certain assumptions which flow from the proposals in the White Paper. However, I should say that many of those assumptions would be appropriate to any system of devolution within our sovereign state.

Those assumptions are, first, that there will be an Assembly with delegated legislative and executive powers constituted by an Act of the sovereign Parliament. May I say with respect to my noble and learned friend Lord Kilbrandon that I believe we in this country know what that is and know what its powers are and how those powers are exercised for whatever reason. It is the Queen in Parliament. Of course, if there were no Assembly this exercise of ours would be quite academic. It is an Assembly that we are considering, not a federal system, nor separation. If it were either of the latter, different considerations would naturally arise.

Secondly, it is a fundamental principle of the proposals that the sovereignty over the whole of the United Kingdom will remain with the Queen in Parliament. Thirdly, whatever precise scope of devolved powers

73

may be determined, they will essentially be limited. Fourthly, according to the proposals in the White Paper, legislation by the Assembly will be subject to Ministerial control on **vires** and to Government and Parliamentary control on policy. Fifthly, there will be considerable areas of law applicable to Scotland as part of the United Kingdom which will remain wholly within the responsibility of Parliament, and such United Kingdom law will be administered by the Scottish judicial system. Sixthly, the law enforcement of all criminal law applicable to Scotland, whatever its source — be it Parliament, or be it the Assembly — will, according to the White Paper proposals, continue to be a function of the United Kingdom Government through the Secretary of State and the Lord Advocate in their respective fields.

The seventh assumption is this. The appointment of the High Court judges, who serve both the Court of Session in civil matters and the High Court of Justiciary in criminal matters, will continue to be made on the recommendation of the Secretary of State and, where appropriate, the Prime Minister. The responsibility for tenure and conditions of office will not be devolved. May I pause there to observe that it would be quite illogical and wrong that appointments of the Queen's judges in Scotland should be made on the recommendations of her appropriate Ministers in the United Kingdom Government, but that such matters as tenure of office and conditions of service should be determined by the Assembly and its Executive.

While the White Paper is silent on the appointment of sheriff principals and sheriffs, we consider it would be wholly wrong in principle if they were treated differently from the High Court judges. They, like us, hold office under warrant from the Sovereign and, with minor exceptions, administer the same law, civil and criminal and from whatever source, as do the High Court judges: and constitutional propriety demands that their appointments should continue to be made by the Sovereign on the recommendation of her appropriate United Kingdom Government Minister. I can tell your Lordships that the sheriff principals, with the exception of my noble and learned friend Lord Wilson of Langside, who could not attend our meeting, are of the same opinion as the High Court judges, standing the present proposals in the White Paper so far as devolved powers are concerned. They depart from us on a question of how there should be a judicial review of **vires**, but I shall deal with that shortly.

The last assumption we make from the proposals in the White Paper is this. The court system in Scotland must be regarded as a unity and responsibility for that system at different levels must not be split. This is recognised in paragraph 149 of the White Paper where it rightly said that the splitting up of responsibility would pose — and, may I interpose, indeed create—

"difficult problems over such matters as jurisdiction, procedure and administration".

It is against that background that I turn to consider, from the constitutional and administrative point of view, the question of where the responsibility

74

for the court system and its administration should lie; whether it should remain with the United Kingdom Government, or be devolved, with or without qualifications, to the Assembly and its Executive. That question is raised in paragraphs 144 to 151 of the White Paper, and is ultimately left open.

The constitutional changes envisaged, if effected, will be a long-term policy. The people talk about the rich heritage of our Scottish law. I agree that it is a rich heritage. But it is our duty not just to look to the past and to the present, but to look to the future; not just to acknowledge and preserve that heritage, but to seek to improve it and hand it down to successors in even greater measure than our predecessors passed it down to us. What we should not do is, for reasons of expediency, derogate from the status of our law or our law courts. What I am about to say, in my personal opinion, should be a test for every function under consideration as to whether or not it should be devolved. But I shall confine and relate it to this question we are now considering of where the responsibility for a court system and its administration should lie. That question should be answered by considering where in the constitutional fabric which is contemplated lies the system which will best protect the status of our courts, the preservation of our standards, and the most effective administration of justice in the interests of the people of Scotland, for whose benefit the whole legal system should be devised.

The answer should not lie in lumping this function into a package deal, whether of a maximum or a minimum nature, as a compromise, or for expediency, or for political reasons, if the merits of the issue dictate that it should go elsewhere. It is the considered view of the Scottish High Court judges that the answer lies in accordance with the second alternative set out in paragraph 150 of the White Paper. I wish to remind your Lordships what that paragraph says, in the alternative:

"it is arguable that the courts are essential elements in the core of constitutional unity of the United Kingdom and in the fabric of law and order; and that since they have to deal with disputes involving both devolved and non-devolved law, they should not be the responsibility of an Assembly which has no functions in the non-devolved fields. The same factors of public policy and national security which are relevant to the police and prosecution functions . . . point towards maintaining United Kingdom responsibility for the courts and their jurisdiction, administration and procedure."

May I try to develop that? I have prefaced what I have to say on this by asserting that in a social democracy such as ours the courts and their administration should be as independent of the Executive as possible. Under the proposals, however altered or modified they might be, our courts will be administering United Kingdom law, and our own common law which, in many cases, marches in parallel with the English common law; community law, as well as legislation passed by the Assembly. In civil matters there will still be a right of appeal to your Lordships' House.

75

Nothing should be done to derogate from the status of our courts. Believing, as we do, that the courts and their administration should remain the responsibility of the sovereign Parliament, we tender arguments both of principle and of practical considerations to support that view. The principle is that the provision, maintenance and oversight of a judicial system in constitutional terms should be a function of the sovereign power, and that power after devolution will still be the Queen in Parliament. To give that function to a delegated body with limited powers which do not embrace the wide spectrum of the work of the courts would not only offend against the principle but might well lower, or appear to lower, the status of our courts in comparison with comparable courts in England. From the practical angle, the judicial system of Scotland must continue to be, in terms of structure, inter-related jurisdiction and procedures, both suitable for and capable of discharging the whole responsibilities of the system; that is, the administration of the whole law applicable to Scotland, which will consist, as I have said, of United Kingdom law, our common law, Community law and Acts of the Assembly in the devolved fields.

The court system in Scotland at each of its levels, and the jurisdictional and procedural relationship between the courts of different levels, can be considered properly only in the context of the totality of the functions it must discharge. The Court of Session (that is, the High Court judges), by acts of sederunt, prescribes the procedure for civil causes of all kinds in the Court of Session and in the sheriff court. The High Court of Justiciary (that is, the High Court judges), by acts of adjournal, regulates for all the criminal courts of Scotland on all matters of procedure not otherwise prescribed by Statute. In their capacity as judges of appeal these same High Court judges have constantly under review the work of all the courts in Scotland. They are accordingly, I would suggest, in the best position to see the work of all the courts in operation and to see whether procedural changes are necessary.

The Lord President of the Court of Session exercises powers of appointment to all kinds of statutory tribunals. I do not want to weary your Lordships, but am merely trying to illustrate the extent to which the administration of justice in Scotland at present is integrated and is regulated and controlled by the court system itself, free from Executive interference. It is true that the Executive is responsible for providing the staff and the buildings, but otherwise the administration of justice and the court system in Scotland is very much where it ought to be — within the hands of the court itself. It seems inevitably to follow from these factors and considerations that the system should remain with the Government and Parliament if the integrity of that system and its ability to discharge properly its functions are not to be impaired.

Power to innovate fundamentally in matters of the powers, jurisdiction and procedure of the courts within the system in any way which might disturb the broad relationship of these courts to each other, and the relative standing of these courts as courts of the United Kingdom, should not be confided to a subordinate authority with responsibility for only one of the sources of the law which the courts will administer. This, I must point out, will in no way derogate from the power of an Assembly to legislate on substantive law in devolved fields; but the suggestion from various sources (some of whom should have known better) that some, if not many, of these powers of the court should be transferred to an Assembly or to a member of its Executive, however designed, be he lawyer or be he layman, could be destructive of a system which has stood the test of time and kept it virtually free and independent of the Executive.

May I now, very briefly I trust, refer to a somewhat related matter. Paragraph 163 of the White Paper states that the Government provisionally favour devolving to an Assembly power to legislate about control of the distinctly Scottish legal profession. I am not quite sure what "control" in that context means, and I am sure we should all like to have it made more clear. The legal profession performs a vital role in the administration of justice in Scotland. In particular, the Court of Session and the High Court of Justiciary depend, in the proper discharge of their functions and in the interpretation, administration and development of the law, upon the professional assistance of members of the Faculty of Advocates. The Faculty of Advocates is indeed an integral part of the College of Justice in Scotland, and control of it has always been vested in the court. In the opinion of the judges, the legal profession in its two distinct branches, in so far as it discharges functions in and connected with litigation, is so inextricably linked with the judicial system itself that responsibility and control of the profession in its relationship with the judicial system must lie where responsibility for that system and its administration lies.

May I lastly now turn to the question of **vires**. I gather from the debate in another place that that question is now very open; and it has been adverted to and criticised by various speakers tonight, particularly by the noble and learned Lord, Lord Hailsham of Saint Marylebone, my noble and learned friend Lord Kilbrandon, the noble Lord, Lord Hughes, and the noble Baroness, Lady Tweedsmuir. Accordingly, I do not want to go over the points that they made, but may I say that the idea that the ultimate decision on a matter of **vires** should rest with a Minister of the Crown is one that offends what we regard as all constitutional propriety.

In spite of the checks proposed while any Bill is going through the Assembly to satisfy the Assembly about its **vires**, and whatever checks may thereafter be made by a Minister of the Crown, there may be cases, even if they occur rarely, where the Assembly Acts exceed, at least in certain of their provisions, the powers devolved by the devolution Statute, or where conflict emerges between the provisions of the United Kingdom Statutes and Assembly Acts. It would seem contrary to sound constitutional principle and, one would think, wise public policy, that any person entitled to invoke the jurisdiction of the courts whose rights are affected by provisions which, **ex hypothesi**, are **ultra vires**, should be denied the protection of the courts. To admit the right of challenge would have the clear advantage of securing respect for the constitutional arrangements embodied in the devolution Statute, and may result in the development and acknowledgment of a body of principles governing the boundaries of the respective competences of Parliament and the

Assembly.

Let me deal with two arguments levelled against this. The first is simply the question that **vires** being decided by a Minister would produce finality and not hamper good government. I think that what was said by my noble and learned friend Lord Kilbrandon on that subject is the short and complete answer. Secondly, it has been said by a Minister in another place that since the **vires** of an Act of Parliament cannot be challenged in court, why should the Acts of Assembly be in a different position? He was not comparing like with like. It may be true of sovereign legislation passed by a sovereign legislative body; it is not true of Acts passed by a devolved legislative body whose powers are written into a constitution enacted in legislation by the parent legislature. It is, in our submission, in exactly the same position as legislation of subordinate nature which has been passed and always been subject to challange in the courts on the question of **vires.**

Nor do we believe that the question of **vires** should be examined in a vacuum by some judicial body. This is where we part company with the sheriffs principal. We have never believed in Scotland in courts setting up theoretical rules or making theoretical decisions which have to be followed in practical cases. We do not have McNaughten Rules or Judges' Rules. We believe that the law can best be determined, enunciated and applied through principles which have been determined from practical problems and considerations brought before the courts. With the best will in the world, the academic exercise might overlook some practical point not envisaged by the draftsman or spotted during the exercise. We accordingly believe that there should be written into devolution Statute an express provision that the **vires** of an Assembly Act can be challenged in court by a litigant. If that principle is established, the mechanics of how it would operate in practice in different cases could no doubt be left to be worked out by the courts themselves.

My Lords, I apologise for detaining your Lordships at this late hour with such a long speech, but I should point out that judges do not have any public relations organisation through which they can make known their views. It is very seldom that they are called upon to express a collective view. In my 22 years' practice on the bench this is the first time that this has happened. The only forum we have, because we cannot use the media, is the bench — and that is designed for other purposes. May I make this appeal, having put on public record in the only way we can the views of the High Court judges, that if these views commend themselves, not only to your Lordships but to others who are responsible for the ultimate decision on these matters, we feel that the status of our institutions and the nature of their administration will be preserved in a manner which the alternative might easily destroy.

D.N. MacCormick

This essay is a restatement of an argument which I advanced in two articles in **The Scotsman** on 5th and 6th February 1976. Since it follows the original text very closely I must at the outset record my gratitude to the editor of **The Scotsman** for permission to reproduce it in this form. The occasion of the original articles was the speech by Lord Wheatley on the Devolution White Paper   . My aim is to contest the arguments advanced by Lord Wheatley. Against his proposition I wish to argue that the main legislative responsibilities for the administration of justice in Scotland ought to be devolved to the proposed Scottish Assembly. I contend that there are strong positive reasons for devolving these responsibilities and that these reasons outweigh the contrary arguments put in Lord Wheatley's speech.

Since his speech is reprinted in full in the present volume, I have refrained from giving references to the **Hansard** text. It will appear readily enough in what follows whether or not I have identified accurately, and dealt fairly with, the principal points in issue.

At the outset it must be acknowledged that Lord Wheatley spoke with the concurrence and prior approval of the whole superior judiciary of Scotland. What is more, both by virtue of his position as Lord Justice Clerk and of his personal eminence and his many contributions to public affairs he is entitled to the highest respect. In venturing to contest his arguments, I am more than conscious of the weight of authority which supports them, and I do so only with the respect which is due to that authority. I am also conscious that the Faculty of Advocates in a memorandum to the Secretary of State concerning the White Paper (published on 8th March 1976) took a similar line to Lord Wheatley's on material points; but I am fortified by the views   expressed by the Law Society of Scotland in its memorandum of 8th January 1976.

One final word to conclude these introductory remarks: my own experience has been as a purely academic lawyer, and if direct experience of the practical, day-to-day administration of justice in Scotland were thought a necessary qualification for expressing an opinion on the present question, I would have to admit myself disqualified. What is more I am a member of, indeed a prospective Parliamentary candidate for, the Scottish National Party. If the arguments which follow fall short of their intended objectivity, the source of their bias is at least plainly declared.

As Lord Wheatley said, it is "the merits of the issue" which matter above all else, not any question of personalities or prejudices. To those merits I now turn; and shall treat firstly of the arguments of principle in favour of devolving legislative responsibility for the administration of civil and criminal justice in Scotland to the Scottish Assembly, secondly of the reasons of practical consequences which also favour that policy, and thirdly of the contrary arguments put by Lord Wheatley.

The context in which the question falls to be debated is one of proposals for devolution, so it is important to remember the essential logic of devolution. Whatever responsibilities in the way of legislation or administration are conferred on the Scottish Assembly or Scottish Executive, there remains in the U.K. Parliament the ultimate overriding power of the supreme legislature. The problematic aspect of devolution is to set the dividing line between what matters are transferred (subject to that ultimate power) and what matters are retained within the direct competence of the sovereign Parliament.

The dividing line which the White Paper aimed to establish — whether successfully or not — sets on one side all matters which are of specifically Scottish concern, except in so far as independent Scottish action might adversely affect the wider British constitutional economic or political systems. Responsibility for all matters falling on the other side of the line — matters of general British interest or concern — should be retained at Westminster.

Two essential reasons of principle are advanced in support of that proposal for devolution in the White Paper. There is the democratic principle that those who exercise public power ought to be answerable to those over whom that power is exercised and that the people specifically concerned with any issue ought to be free to determine and pursue their own priorities on a matter which **ex hypothesi** is not of vital concern to anyone else (see, e.g. paragraph 14 of the White Paper). But that principle presupposes some basis on which to determine units of government, for which reference may be made to the other principle which, in no tendentious sense, I would call the "nationalistic principle". As the White Paper says (para. 11), "Within the United Kingdom Scotland and Wales have kept their own identities, with distinctive elements of tradition, culture and institutions". The principle is that democratic political institutions ought to be established through which can be expressed such national identities as those of Scotland and Wales.

In terms of the dividing line established, it is difficult to conceive of an issue which more closely concerns the well-being of the community of Scotland than the administration within it of civil and criminal justice. Subject to a point made in para. 150 of the White Paper and discussed in the third section of this essay, the good administration of justice in Scotland is of predominantly, or even purely, Scottish concern. Both the democratic and the nationalistic principles therefore point unequivocally towards devolvement of legislative responsibility in this sphere — and also, so far as relevant, of Executive responsibility.

The conception of "responsibility" here involved is entirely different from that of "control", the use of which in the White Paper and elsewhere Lord Wheatley so justifiably deplored in his speech. Responsibility in a legislative or governmental sphere is often best exercised by abstention from, not assertion of, "control".

The force of our arguments from principle ought not to be under-estimated. The two principles involved appear to command the support of a large and diversely constituted majority of people in Scotland, as well as

80

having informed the Government's approach to its devolution proposals. All recent opinion polls suggest that a majority of Scottish Conservative, Labour and Liberal voters favours legislative devolution for Scotland. For that devolutionist majority of those voters, these principles must be presumed to be implicit in their preferences. And certainly the nationalistic principle is for them far from absolute; it is qualified by reason of the assertion of a British as well as a Scottish identity, whence the insistence on maintaining overall political and economic unity. For members and at least some supporters of the Scottish National Party the two principles are not so qualified, and are taken to justify a policy of Scottish independence. From that point of view, devolution is seen as but a staging post on a progress to the recovery by Scotland of an entire responsibility for all its communal affairs.

Despite such differences of emphasis and of political aims, our statement of the principles can fairly be said to capture the gist of an opinion shared by the great mass of the Scottish electorate. Moreover, such principles deserve the assent of all those who value democratic forms of society within historically and culturally distinctive communities. As such they constitute the strongest of prima facie reasons for the devolution of responsibility for the court system.

But certainly general principles do not of themselves settle concrete cases. At best, they point towards solutions which should be adopted only if there are also practical reasons in favour, and if there are not decisive counterweighing considerations of practice and of principle.

II

What then are the practical considerations in favour of devolving to the Scottish legislature responsibility for the administration of justice in Scotland? One highly important one is the practicability of securing legislative changes when these are desired. Consider, for example, the recent report of the Thomson Committee, which proposed far-reaching and controversial changes in highly important aspects of our criminal procedure. Such proposals ought in their very nature to be a focus of careful and widespread discussion and debate in a democratic and civilised community.

In such debate much weight must be given to the opinion of those who are qualified and experienced in the working of the present system; but in the end of the day even the experts may be overridden.

If responsibility for the administration of justice were a devolved matter, the crucial debates would indeed take place in the Scottish Assembly among the elected representatives of those whose whose lives and liberties would be directly affected by the adoption or rejection of the proposals. It is hard to believe that there would be a long delay in finding parliamentary time to debate so vital an issue, or in finding time for such legislation (if any) as might be favoured by a majority.

By contrast, an effect of substantial devolution, must be to diminish (even beyond the present small quantum) the amount of precious

81

legislative time which the United Kingdom Parliament would be prepared to devote to legislation exclusively Scottish in character. (Be it noted that the same is true of the legislation concerning the ancient Universities of Scotland). So it would be increasingly difficult to secure adequate debating of such a matter at Westminster or, a fortiori, to achieve legislation when desired.

It might in those circumstances prove most expeditious to tack reforming legislation for the Scottish courts on to parallel or similar Bills concerning the administration of justice in England (or England and Wales). In which context, although in an opposite sense, one can only repeat Lord Wheatley's apprehensions concerning policies which "might well lower, or appear to lower, the status of our courts in comparison with comparable courts in England".

That apart, one can urge again the importance of the existence of an articulate, aware, and open-minded "legislative public opinion" (Dicey's phrase) upon such issues in Scotland. It is something of which we had far too little in Scotland for far too long. It is difficult to have legislative public opinion without a legislature, or on issues for which the legislatures in existence either lack responsibility or lack time and interest for full and searching debate.

The same argument, mutatis mutandis, can be applied across the whole spectrum of the administration of justice, of private law, of criminal law, and of a good deal of administrative law. These have come to be seen far too much as being issues for the experts alone; yet they profoundly affect the lives and happiness of the whole community. On the whole, Westminster has lacked time for, and five hundred and fourteen M.P.s have quite reasonably lacked serious interest in, Scottish law reform. One way to create a democratic awareness of Scots law and its importance to people is to create an elected Scottish Assembly with responsibility — again I stress "responsibility" — in relation to it.

To take a final example, another potentially controversial question of considerable importance to the general public, concerns jurisdiction in consistorial causes. Should divorce remain within the jurisdiction of the Court of Session, centralised in Edinburgh; or should jurisdiction be conferred on the Sheriff Court? It is difficult to believe that English M.P.s would be eager after devolution to have this debated in Westminster, with whatever result, the English legal system having some years since settled for a considerable degree of decentralisation of such matters to County Courts.

Whatever be the better view on this question, the answer is of considerable concern to people in Scotland, and of no concern at all to anyone else, except in a general and speculative way. It is again hard to think of a matter more appropriate on practical grounds, as well as on democratic grounds, for transfer to the competence of the Scottish Assembly.

It appears that there are strong reasons of practice as well as of principle in favour of devolving responsibility for the legislative framework within which the courts and the legal profession exercise their functions in the administration of justice. Are these outweighed by counter-arguments? To that question I shall turn next, with a view to giving full consideration to the arguments advanced by Lord Wheatley.

The text of his speech, as I read it, seems to contain six main points of argument. Notwithstanding the profound respect which I owe to their author and his authority, I have not been answered by them, for reasons which will appear.

First, there is a practical argument rather hinted at than stated by Lord Wheatley; the Scottish Assembly might legislate badly, asserting ill-judged "control" over the system, and adversely affecting the quality of the justice administered there.

So it might. But to be a democrat is to believe that (a) such decisions ought to be taken by the elected representatives of the people directly affected by the decisions, who are the ultimate judges of right and wrong in the matter; and (b) that being so, the system builds in the best available, though not an infallible, protection against wrong decisions. The same is true of the U.K. Parliament, which by the same token might occasionally pass ill-advised legislation itself and which could, in any event override Scottish Assembly legislation in any extreme case under a devolutionary system .

Secondly, there is Lord Wheatley's argument that it would be "quite illogical and wrong" to devolve legislative responsibility for the court system so long as the appointment by the Queen of her judges in Scotland remained (by convention) a matter upon which Ministers in the U.K. Cabinet gave the decisive advice.

But the reason (whether or not it is accepted as good or compelling) for retaining the function of advice on Scottish judicial appointments within the U.K. Ministry is, presumably, to avoid the risk of appointment of persons thought likely to favour the political or other ambitions of the Scottish Executive for the time being. Since the judiciary will have to pronounce on the validity of acts of the Scottish Executive (and perhaps Assembly as well), that may be thought necessary to securing the independence of the judiciary. As to that, it may be pointed out that the same applies to the U.K. Government, and that twice in the past 11 years decisions of the courts in Scottish litigation adverse to the Government have been reversed by retroactive legislation.

But the securing of the personal independence of the judiciary by the appointment of impartial individuals of the highest legal eminence is surely a policy materially different from the policy or policies involved in the provision of a legislative framework for the fair and expeditious disposal of questions raised before those eminent and impartial judges. There is a connection of course, but in my submission not so close and intimate as to make it "quite illogical and wrong" to have different authorities responsible for the different questions.

Thirdly, Lord Wheatley argues that the court system in Scotland must be regarded as a unity, and responsibility for that system at different levels must not be split (namely as between High Court and Sheriff Court levels) . I respectfully agree on this point, which is however neutral as between allocating such overall responsibility to Edinburgh or to

Westminster (given that the power of appointment of judges is a separate, or separable matter).

Fourthly, there is the argument stated in para. 150 of the White Paper, and adopted by Lord Wheatley; the argument which stresses that "the courts are essential elements in the core of constitutional unity of the United Kingdom and in the fabric of law and order". Here arises the caveat mentioned earlier; if an overriding value is set on "political and economic unity", then the court system may be conceived as an element in political though not (in any direct sense) economic unity.

I do not share that political premise, which may render my argument suspect upon this point. But I must say that I do not believe that to devolve legislative responsibility for the administration of justice would tend of itself to promote the termination of the existing Parliamentary Union. If anything, the reverse might be true, in the sense that resentment would probably be occasioned among the Scottish electorate if it were faced with a legislative assembly powerless to reform Scottish criminal procedure or civil procedure — especially if Westminster lacked the time or the interest to do so.

I am bound to say that the issue whether the kind of political and economic unity within which the peoples of the British Isles must live entails sharing a single sovereign Parliament with authority over a quasi-unitary judicial system, is a different question altogether from the immediate question whether or not to devolve legislative responsibility for the present Court system. It is a different question, and one which will in the end be answered quite independently of the present answer to the present question.

Fifthly, there is the argument, stated in the White Paper and by Lord Wheatley, that the laws to be administered by the Scottish courts will include legislation of the U.K. Parliament and of E.E.C. organs as well as Scottish common law and Assembly legislation; and that therefore the Assembly ought not to have the power to set the legislative framework for Courts whose law will emanate from all such sources.

It may be submitted in answer that whatever the sources of the law administered by any courts, one can best secure the efficient administration of all that law by allocating legislative responsibility to those bodies having the time and interest necessary for a careful and searching consideration of all relevant facts and circumstances.

In many matters — all day to day matters — that argues for the vesting of (delegated) legislative power in the courts themselves. As Lord Wheatley said, that is now the case, and ought to remain the case.

But there remain the wider, and more fundamental, questions which have been thought hitherto more appropriate to legislation by an elected body than to delegated legislation by the judiciary. As to these, the body which will qualify on 'time and interest' grounds will surely be the Scottish Assembly; no doubt the Westminster Parliament could be relied upon to use its built-in overriding power if the Assembly sought to use such power as a back door for invading the preserves of reserved legislative power.

Finally, we must consider Lord Wheatley's argument based on "the principle . . "that the provision, maintenance and oversight of a judicial system in constitutional terms should be a function of the Sovereign power, and that power after devolution will still be the Queen in Parliament". Legal theories based on the idea of sovereignty are perhaps less widely accepted now than once they were. But even if the principle is accepted without demur, it is not clear that the conclusion drawn from it is a necessary deduction. The Sovereign power must provide, maintain and oversee the judicial system. But would it be a breach of the principle if the sovereign devolved the function wholly or partly to a subordinate but democratically elected Assembly? Would it be so even if the members of that Assembly would have the most direct and material concern to secure the continued operation of a just and efficient judicial system, such as we have in Scotland?

With deep respect, I do not believe that these questions must be answered in the affirmative. In the circumstances envisaged, delegation by the sovereign to a devolved but democratic authority is probably the best way in which it can fulfil its duty in the matter. The principle may be an absolute one, but the guidance which it provides in this context is certainly not absolute or unequivocal. Indeed as our two most noted proponents of theories of sovereignty, Austin and Bentham, observed, a sovereign body is necessarily such that it can act through delegates or not as it sees fit. Whether or not it should use a delegate for some particular purpose is a question the answer to which should be determined on the basis of a rounded view of the greatest overall advantage. And, by definition, the Sovereign power retains the ability to intervene if the devolved legislature should behave with manifest frivolity, ineptitude or bad purpose.

For the reasons here stated, I should submit that a rounded view of the greatest overall advantage does favour devolving legislative responsibility for the Court system, and indeed for as much as possible of private law, criminal law and administrative law. The principles and practical reasons in favour of doing so are not outweighed by the arguments of principle and practice which point in the opposite direction. Rather, they outweigh them.

At the bottom of the whole debate is a concern to preserve the impartiality and independence of the Courts and of the legal profession. That shines out from the speech of Lord Wheatley and from the memoranda presented by the Faculty of Advocates and the Law Society of Scotland. These are values, it is sometimes said, which must be kept out of politics and preserved from political interference, and the fear of such interference may have motivated some of the concern about devolution of the matters here under consideration. The truth, surely, is that such values are not non-political, but supremely political. The independence and integrity of the Court system are vital to the health of the body politic and to the security of every individual within it. As such they are supreme political values which ought to be accepted as being beyond mere party political controversy.

I have confidence in the political maturity and wisdom of the community of Scotland. If it is the case that the people of Scotland are not able to respect these values and to hold them above party controversy, then they are not fit for any degree of self-government. But the devolution proposals are founded on the supposition that they are fit for that, and the supposition seems well founded. Even from the point of view of someone who accepted the White Paper scheme for devolution as basically sufficient and satisfactory, the case for including responsibility for the courts and the law within the scheme would be, in my submission, overwhelmingly strong.

Devolving the Universities

PROBLEMS and PROSPECTS

J.McIntyre

The arguments for and against the devolution of the universities of Scotland, propounded with such vigour and conviction by both sides to the controversy, in particular over the past two years, are now passing into the folk-lore of the great debate on the future of our nation. In fact the arguments have become almost stylised and legendary so that they can be rehearsed rather like a liturgy. They are public property, to be used by anyone who wishes to raise his voice on this subject. So there would seem to be little excuse for taking the matter up once again were it not my belief that we are in danger of accepting a major fallacy. The fallacy is that it is sound and permissible educational policy to regard the future of the universities in Scotland as insulatable from the future of other Scottish institutions. Whitehead used to speak of the fallacy of misplaced concreteness, that is the error of assuming that one sector of reality could be regarded as if it were an entity on its own independent of the rest of reality, and with problems which could be solved without reference to the rest of reality. If we construe our fallacy in psychological terms we can see that it becomes the fantasy of the universities' withdrawal from the real world of Scottish education with its many intractable problems. In moral terms, fallacy and fantasy become irresponsibility if we in the universities think that we can save our own skins and make our universities secure while letting other sectors of education make the best of a bad job. What I propose, therefore, is to try to set the future of the universities within the broader context of education in Scotland.

87

But first of all, piety obliges me to recite the litany not only so that we may have the arguments for and against the devolution of the universities before us from the start, but also because in these arguments the wider issues constantly obtrude. I should add that I have here and elsewhere in this essay drawn upon material which I prepared for a Conference held to mark the tenth anniversary of the Scottish edition of the **Times Educational Supplement** in Edinburgh in June 1975.

Taking the arguments **against,** first, we note that much is made of the buffer role which the national University Grants Committee has played throughout its existence between the universities and the government of the day, so that the idiosyncratic views of any one government and changes of government should not have disruptive effects on university academic programmes. When the question is asked why a Scottish University Grants Committee could not give the same service, the answer is that a local legislature at close range might be constantly prying into priorities and expenditure. Petty animosities might develop and reprisals for disagreement or non-cooperation would in the end curb all freedom and initiative. In other words, we could look forward to nothing but political interference, and a measure of economic control which would lead to the manipulation of academic affairs. Moreover, some people fear that the universities, having been devolved, might be treated less favourably than other institutions of higher education in Scotland. To support their predictions they point to allegations which have been made that the universities are elitist and have in fact in the past been treated too lavishly. In the wider national setting the Scottish universities could count upon the support of their colleagues south of the border to combat any national move to down-grade universities at the expense of other institutions.

It is further contested that creation of a Scottish University Grants Committee separate from an English University Grants Committee would involve the division of what ought to be a unitary university system and create problems for students and staff wishing to move from one country to the other. The Scottish universities would then become regional or even parochial institutions, and would lose that international reputation which association with their sister institutions in the south brings - an argument, incidentally, which is in no way supported by the history of the Scottish universities before the twentieth century. A great deal is made in the case against devolution of the universities of the fact that the research councils make their awards on a national basis and that the Scottish universities if withdrawn from the national system would forfeit their claim and interest, or at best be severely incapacitated in the competition for places and money. It is also assumed that the academic standards of Scottish students would fall because they would face less competition from unusually bright incomers - an assumption which ignores the possibility that Scottish universities might still be attractive to students even after devolution.

The case **for** devolution of the universities is equally detailed: It begins with criticism of the case against. The point is made, for example, that some English universities are very close to the seat of power, whether one puts it in Westminster or in Whitehall. Yet they seem to have suffered
88

neither more or less than the rest of us from the attentions of interfering politicians and civil servants. In other words, proximity to the legislature or the bureaucracy does not seem to matter greatly. Further, in Scotland, quite a few colleges such as the central institutions and the colleges of education are already under the supervision of the Secretary of State or the Scottish Education Department. There is no evidence to suggest that they have surrendered their academic integrity to the state. Perhaps, too, it ought to be said that the existing University Grants Committee is not altogether the buffer that it once was against governmental interest in the universities. The Treasury exerts far greater control over the universities than was ever the case in the boom years, through its financial allocations and so to the University Grants Committee. Not wholly retrievable statements have also been made about the government doing "something more positive in the manpower planning field to guide its choices in the educational field" (Lord Crowther Hunt, quoted in **The Observer,** 25th May 1975).

In short, government interest in universities, whether the government be the present Westminster Parliament or the projected Scottish Assembly, is more likely to be determined by manpower needs, available finance and, one might add, doctrinaire educational policy, than by physical proximity. It has been argued that a devolved Scottish university system would result in the encouragement of Scottish studies in literature, history, art, economics and philosophy, to a degree at present impossible, and would thus halt what has been called "the anglicising of our culture and institutions". I sometimes wonder whether much ought to be made of this argument. Scottish studies have certainly flourished in the University of Edinburgh in recent years and many have received encouragement directly from the University Court. It is hard to imagine that greater encouragement would have come had the universities been financed by a Scottish Assembly. Greater weight ought, on the other hand, to be given to the claim that the unequal yoking of Scottish and English universities as if they were identical partners in a unitary system has sometimes been to the disadvantage of pupils entering university from schools which followed the long-established Scottish custom of offering a broadly based curriculum. Moreover, there is a specifically Scottish tradition of education. This unequal yoking has seriously diminished it in the past thirty years. The devolution controversy has served to bring into fresh focus what Dr G. E. Davie was saying about that tradition in **The Democratic Intellect** fifteen years ago.

Those against the devolution of the Scottish universities seem to have gained a first round advantage, because the White Paper on devolution published in November 1975 excluded the universities from the package. The government has called for submissions on the White Paper and the debate continues, but as yet fresh arguments have not appeared. The thesis which I wish to propound is that not only will no new light be thrown on the issue if we pursue these arguments about it , . . .   , but that we shall run the far greater risk of being satisfied with the arguments offered so far and fail to see that the universities are but one part — albeit a significant even dominant part — of the Scottish educational system. For this reason the crisis in Scottish education is the subject of the second part of my essay. Only if the universities play their part, and use their intellectual resources to the full, will this crisis be resolved to the greater good of Scottish education. The devolution controversy must not be used as a red herring to divert us from making a supreme effort to assist in the solution of this crisis. This is our responsibility just as it is the responsibility of all other educationalists in Scotland.

The shape of the solution which we reach will be determined by four sets of factors and will result from the interplay of these factors upon one another. The strategic place which the universities occupy in this analysis will become clear as we go along. We must begin by considering a number of tensions. The first is caused by the system of admitting to the universities students with many varied, but by implication equal qualifications — S.C.E., G.C.E., diplomas of recognised institutions and certain professional qualifications. The fact that these qualifications are not equal becomes apparent only after the students have arrived. The recent public correspondence over failure rates — a problem which affects all the universities and not just the one which was singled out — is evidence of this tension. It is especially encouraging to learn that the Scottish universities have begun to work out ways of solving this problem. So long as it remains unsolved much distress is likely to occur among undergraduates.

A second tension which is partly responsible for the previous one is to be found in school curricula. These, it seems, are expected to serve what might be thought to be irreconcilable objectives. The first is to provide pupils with the necessary qualifications for university entrance. The second is to offer either a general education or some kind of entrance qualification for non-university education or for some profession. These irreconcilable objectives are sometimes dealt with by choices of subjects; what is not clear is that they can be satisfactorily accommodated within one structure of education. This second tension has also appeared in universities which seem on the one hand intent on giving a general education — the old Scottish M.A. being the classic example — and on the other committed to preparing entrants for several different professions. In this connection it is interesting that the faculty of law which was once very closely related to professional training is now attracting many students who do not intend to take up law as a career, but who see the curriculum of that faculty as providing them with a broadly based education. Ideally these two aims should be combined in universities, but they do from time to time create tension.

"Comprehensive" is rapidly becoming an established attribute of education. Whether or not a school is "comprehensive" determines both the financial aid it receives from the government and its curriculum. Within schools comprehensive education has given substance to the concept of universalism which had already received its form in the raised school-leaving age. But that universalism begins to be at odds with the long-standing elitism of the universities. In the universities the tension has led different people in different directions. Some maintain that the comprehensive principle should be extended to universities; others that selectivity is essential to the success of the universities. In the recent discussions of higher education in Scotland, a great deal has been made of the next tension. That is, the tension between the universities — with their long-standing role in Scottish society, their international status, their clearly defined academic standards and their acknowledged place in the academic structure of Scotland — and the other centres of tertiary education. The role of these other centres has still to be determined by the planners and they have as yet had little opportunity to establish themselves on the international scene or to define with precision the standards which they can reasonably expect from their students. This tension is not simply one of status, or role, or even of universalism versus elitism. It is caused by uncertainty about the function of these different institutions in the community and about the kind of service they should be giving to the young of this nation.

This last reflection takes us at once to a tension of which the universities have become aware in the harsh economic climate of the last three years. It is the tension between a **past** in which the universities had come to regard themselves as largely autonomous within the kindly protectorate of the University Grants Committee, their development following in considerable measure their own assessment of the points at which academic growth should take place and a **present,** in which sharp and at times hostile questions are being asked about their contribution to the community, and about the value of certain kinds of research.

Utilitarian criteria are now beginning to be applied to universities and new responsibilities placed upon them. Whereas in the past the universities concentrated almost exclusively on the admission of school leavers, it is now firmly proposed that they should take responsibility for late entrants to university and for "in-service" and "post-experience" education. This dual commitment creates new problems. What admission criteria should the universities use? Their anxieties may be increased when it is suggested that the term "comprehensive" should be applied to university education.

There is another tension which derives from the simple collocation of the adjectives, big and small, bad and beautiful. We have not yet been able to decide whether the student is better cared for in the small institution, where his identity is immediately clear both to himself and to his tutor, or whether it is now unrealistic to think of any tertiary education — other than that in the liberal arts — except in a large institution which can bear the costs of expensive equipment and the salary rates that go with its maintenance. Happily most universities have stopped playing "the numbers game", but there is a danger of making a virtue of the necessity imposed upon us by economic stringency and of pretending that the size we are (whatever it is) is beautiful.

Polytechnics are becoming popular, particularly south of the border. This development is obviously relevant to Scotland, but it raises an important issue. Is there any place at the tertiary level for the "monotechnic"? Or should all institutions at the tertiary level strive to be poly-disciplinary? The problem is that some universities, having expanded to five or ten thousand, find themselves threatened with fragmentation into faculties which are larger than many tertiary institutions. They are now beginning to wonder whether they are in fact agglomerations of monotechnics. Meanwhile other tertiary institutions are moving in the opposite direction from monotechnic to polytechnic.

Our final tension is an emotional one. On the one hand a certain disenchantment with universities is arising in part because of the employment situation, and in part because of unfavourable publicity about student attitudes and behaviour. On the other hand, many Scottish people have a deeply rooted conviction that universities have a special part to play in the training of the young. Perhaps the tension arises because the universities cannot always be seen clearly to be playing that part.

Before proceeding to the major proposals which form the second part of this essay, I should like to delineate the second set of factors which I believe should determine the shape of tertiary education in Scotland. These are a series of principles which can be derived from the tensions indicated above. For tensions if allowed scope and employed constructively need not inhibit us nor be pathological nor paralysing.

The first principle is that of **continuity.** Pupils should be able to "flow through" the educational process from primary, or even nursery, level to tertiary level. Many schools have now succeeded in eliminating the trauma of the eleven-plus, but it remains for us, particularly in Scotland, to make every effort to deal with the even more serious trauma which occurs when students make the transition from school to university, or worse still, fail to make it. The problem is partly one of entrance standards, but perhaps the closer accommodation of school and university curricula is even more important. At the same time the universities must continue to ensure that people with varied qualifications can enter.

Perhaps the time has come to say firmly that the dichotomy between professional training and general education is a false one. Within higher education, no matter what the institution, educators are failing if all they are providing is the technical ability to do a certain job. Their aim should surely be to foster their students' critical capacities and increase their ability to weigh evidence, perceive general principles, state and argue a case and co-operate with colleagues. The false dichotomy should be replaced therefore with the principle of **professional education.**

The principle of "comprehensive education" ought now to be re-examined to see whether it is relevant to universities. The principle which it enshrines is more readily identifiable as "openness", as willingness to explore more scientifically than we have hitherto, the concept of "educability". There are certain disciplines which are available at university and not at school, and in which mature students often demonstrate ability which cannot be correlated with their entrance qualifications or lack of them. For such disciplines, I am prepared to argue that the sole qualifications should be the capacity to read and to express oneself in writing. However, these qualifications are perhaps rarer than we think.

The integration of all Scottish tertiary education has now become a clamant necessity. By that term I do not mean "homogenisation", or the consumption of the less by the greater, or the reduction of all to some dead uniformity. An alternative word would be co-ordination. How this co-ordination might work is a subject to which I return. It would be good too, if the community role of all sectors of tertiary education could now be accepted and accepted willingly. Nostalgia for the days when we could follow the argument wherever it led, regardless of time and expense is misplaced. The ivory tower is no more, and perhaps that is a good thing. What we do, in the universities in particular, has to be seen to have some significance for society, either in the short or the long term. If it doesn't,we have to give serious consideration to the question of why we do it. Unless carefully watched, research can become a very costly form of self-indulgence.

May we say once and for all that there is no optimal size for an institution at the tertiary level? In fact, it is best to have a mixture of different sizes of institution to allow for idiosyncrasies both in discipline and personality. Small and big may be either bad or beautiful; and you will not know till you try.

The third set of factors to affect the shape of tertiary education in Scotland are the constraints within which planning must take place. While the tensions outlined above may actually help us to be creative and to develop a set of working principles, it would be unrealistic not to acknowledge that we shall have to operate within certain very strict limits. It is to these that I now turn.

We have already come sharply up against the control imposed upon the universities by the fixed financial allocation allowed for the forthcoming year 1976-77. We have grown accustomed to a reduction in the number of our staff, but we shall now have to face an educational "squeeze" as we realise the cost of the multiplicity of honours and joint-honours courses which we have devised in the past decade. A hard-headed assessment of priorities and preferences will be essential. Financial stringency is the first constraint.

A second constraint is that projections about the number of entrants into the tertiary education in the next decade are uncertain. Indications are that the numbers will drop because of a decrease in the population aged 18-21, but against such a decrease we have to set a possible growth in in-service trainees and late educands.

The third constraint will be our own capacity to plan. In the hard times ahead our planning will need to be much more accurate than it was in the days of plenty, when we received one year what we failed to get the year before. But the years of plenty yielded no wisdom; we went in fits and starts, living somewhere in the middle-space between our hands and our mouths.

And finally our development will be bounded by the philosophy of tertiary education that we devise or fail to devise. It is surely a major lacuna in our self-knowledge that in a decade of rapid expansion in the universities we never really knew what we were doing. We never worked out a comprehensive philosophy of education. We added piece to piece with the abandon of opportunists. Now that that era is ended, perhaps we will take time to discover what we did do, and to introduce some fundamental concepts and structure into what is still too often chaotic.

We now come to the fourth set of factors which may have some bearing on the future of tertiary education in Scotland, namely, proposals for reshaping it.

Before the publication of the White Paper on devolution many people seemed to feel that if the universities were excluded from the plan and remained with the national University Grants Committee then somehow the Scottish universities were free to continue as before, cocooned and isolated from the rest of Scottish higher education. In the event, the universities were excluded, but the controversy which their exclusion aroused led to one of the most interesting discussions in Scottish educational circles for many years. Many people feel, indeed many are convinced, that the universities cannot for much longer disregard what is happening in the parallel institutions. Here, I am prepared to argue, is an opportunity for them to assume the role of leadership. Or if that sounds too imperialistic, they could at least indicate their willingness to share in solving what is after all a common problem! There are encouraging signs that they may soon do so.

Let us begin with the schools for they featured quite extensively in my analysis of the tensions within Scottish education. Clearly some schools have solved the problem of the smooth ''through-flow'' from school to university, though even in these there are each year pupils who do not conform to the pattern which the school has achieved, and for whom some alternative approach to the university would be useful. It would be folly to suggest any changes in the normal pattern of approach which such schools have achieved.

Certain other schools might welcome a reappraisal of what takes place in their upper years. Some have made determined efforts to introduce sixth form studies, but have found their efforts unrewarding. Some pupils who still have highers to take to meet university entrance requirements mix sixth form studies with preparation for highers, taking the latter more seriously than the former. Others embarking on sixth form studies with good intentions in August, find their interest draining away after the universities issue unconditional acceptances in February or March. To meet what is now quite a general malaise about the sixth form, and for the benefit of schools other than those mentioned in the previous paragraph — a very important exception — it is proposed that school education should end in fifth year, the normal year for the taking of highers by the average to good pupil. The tertiary colleges should then make available courses of two or three years duration, which would cater (as they have done so excellently in the past) for those who leave school without achieving university entrance, or who are still undecided about their academic future and wish to take qualifications other than those available at school.

This reference to colleges suggests that we now look at the role which they should have in a restructured tertiary scheme. I do so with a certain diffidence and only because I feel that their position ought to be enhanced and the role they play clearly defined. Obviously they will wish to continue with the professional training which they have traditionally supplied, though they themselves are moving in the direction of what we earlier called **professional education.** In recognition of their Scottish character, they might be persuaded to include in their curricula courses in logic, metaphysics and ethics, as was the case for many decades in the old Scottish universities in times when students were much younger than they are on average today. But if we follow up the proposal in the previous paragraph, we could think of them continuing with the students who came in from school right through to graduation level.

The term "graduation level" is used advisedly, because they will be, as some already are, degree-conferring bodies. But their great strength would lie in the fact that they would maintain open access for students from school or for late educands, while still holding to rigorous standards of exit and graduation. But the restructuring would not be complete if we did not integrate the colleges explicitly with the universities, extending an arrangement which already obtains between certain colleges and universities in some of the science and technology subjects. This integration would take the form of permitting students from the colleges at the end of the second or third year to move over into the university for, say, the last two years of an honours degree. Equally, a student from the university might take the reverse step. One condition of such an arrangement would be that the universities and the colleges collaborate in the planning of courses. Such collaboration may in any case be forced upon us by financial stringency or adopted by us on the grounds of common sense.

This system would require considerable goodwill from many quarters. Indeed success would probably only be possible if the participating bodies were represented on the supervisory group, which some have already christened "The Scottish Academic Council". Such a council would need to be supported at the local level by governing bodies such as the present University Courts with lay, staff and student membership and by some academic bodies with responsibility solely for curricula, examinations, admissions and so on. If devolution were extended to cover all Scottish academic institutions, then the council I have suggested could well become a Standing Committee on Education, to which a Scottish University Grants Committee would have to be answerable. It would be quite unrealistic to expect that a Scottish University Grants Committee could remain autonomous, in a way which does not hold even for the present University Grants Committee, vis-a-vis the Department of Education and Science.

If, however, the Scottish tertiary institutions are unwilling for one reason or another to set up something like the organisation described above, or to show the spirit of co-operation which such a scheme presupposes, then three courses are open for consideration. First, we may just await the outcome of the parliamentary debate on devolution. If we do this we shall have to allow the processes of innovation, should the universities be devolved, to produce some plan or other or if the universities are excluded

95

resign ourselves to the **status quo.** Either way, I see little hope of improvement in Scottish higher education. Secondly, we may adopt the proposal of the Scottish executive of the National Union of Students made in March 1975 that an independent public inquiry be instituted to examine the purpose, administration and finance of the Scottish post-school system, and make recommendations to a future Assembly. But that will not do for several reasons. To begin with, it is totally inadvisable to focus the examination upon the possibility of some as yet non-existent Assembly, with as yet controversial powers in the educational field. We need the examination of tertiary education **now,** not a year or two years from now. Next, the findings of such a public inquiry would in no way bind the Assembly. The findings of the Reporter in the public inquiry in the case of the Turnhouse runway were disregarded by the Secretary of State; and what one man can do 142 can do. The public inquiry is not a medium of democratic decision; and tertiary education, because of the future and destiny of the thousands of young people involved, must not be left to the arbitrariness of such an idiosyncratic process.

Accordingly, I can see no satisfactory alternative in our present plight but to demand some kind of Royal Commission to deal with the issues discussed in this essay. I suggested a possible remit for such a commission at the Times Educational Supplement (Scotland) Conference mentioned earlier and I see no reason to alter it now. The situation has not improved in the year since that conference, and in many ways it has deteriorated. The remit would run as follows:

(1) To define the aims of education in modern society, and in particular in Scotland;

(2) To outline how these aims might be achieved through schools, colleges and universities;

(3) To restructure the relations which at present obtain among these agents of education with a view to co-ordinating them to allow of transfer from the one to the other;

(4) To take account of the possible ways in which the history of thought concerning educational theory in Scotland might be of value in the present situation;

(5) To make provision for the admission to the system of those who wish education at a mature stage in life and are without the normal qualifications;

(6) To include in the system provision for post-experience and in-service training;

(7) To design constitutional arrangements for the supervision of this co-ordinated system of tertiary education, both at the national and at the local level;

(8) To define ways in which a Scottish tertiary system would relate to the educational systems of other parts of the United Kingdom.

The   findings of such a commission would have to have a more binding power than a public inquiry; and provision would be required to ensure that we did not have a repetition of the runway debacle.

If there is a single unifying theme in this essay it is that the educational crisis in Scotland which affects not only the tertiary institutions but also the schools will not suddenly be resolved, whichever way the question of the devolution of the universities goes. The issues are far too important and too complicated. They should in all fairness be given proper attention and no longer be treated as if they were of minor consequence in some larger game. Indeed the Scottish education system is in danger of being used as a negotiating piece in what are increasingly cynical and squalid manoeuvres.

Would Scotland be economically better off as an independent country? Since the discovery of large deposits of oil and gas off the Scottish coast this question has been an important part of the political debate. We republish here C. R. Smallwood's controversial article in which he stated the economic case against independence. When Smallwood's article appeared in the **Scotsman** it led to a prolonged and diverse correspondence. One of Smallwood's most convincing antagonist was Professor D. I. MacKay. Professor MacKay has restated his argument for us and we have given each the chance to reply to the other. So the main articles are followed by two postscripts. We are grateful to the editor of the **Scotsman** for his permission to reprint the original article.

The Economics of Independence

C.R.Smallwood D.I.MacKay

One of the most striking aspects of the political debate in Scotland a present is the commonly held belief that — whether or not independence is desirable on other grounds — Scotland would be much better of economically if she opted for independence.

The Nationalists, of course, have a vested interest in arguing that if only there were a Scottish Government, with access to the untold riches of the North Sea, Scotland's economic difficulties would soon be over. What is more surprising however is that the major political parties in Scotland have not yet presented any systematic rebuttal of the Nationalists economic case.

From the point of view of the Government's devolution proposals, it is unfortunate that such a rebuttal has not been made. For as long as the view prevails that independence would bestow enormous economic benefits on Scotland, it is inevitable that whatever the devolution White Paper contains, it will be regarded as an inadequate response to Scotland's needs and aspirations. If those proposals are to receive a fair hearing, therefore, it is essential to take a clear and dispassionate look at what, in economic terms, independence would really entail.

The fact is that a serious analysis of the economic prospects of an independent Scotland does not indicate that in economic terms independence is clearly Scotland's best option. The economic gains which independence might bring would be much less than commonly imagined, and the economic costs and difficulties and risks, hardly ever mentioned, would be considerable. Consequently, there is no necessity for those people who are Scottish and who wish to remain citizens of the UK to concede the economic argument to the other side. The purpose of this article is to explain why any analysis of the economic consequences of independence has to come to terms with a number of basic questions. Granted that Scottish independence would have to be negotiated, what would the terms of an independence settlement be? Would Scotland remain a part of the UK monetary union, or would there be a separate Scottish currency with its own rate of exchange? How much would the oil revenues really be worth? While we cannot give definite answers to these questions, it seems reasonable to make the following suppositions — which are, if anything, rather favourable to the separatist case.

Oil: No one knows what will happen to oil prices in the coming years. There are persuasive arguments both ways. It is reasonable therefore to think in terms of a constant price, and consequently to have in mind a figure of £3,000 million for North Sea oil revenues.

Division of oil revenues: While international legal conventions would seem to give Scotland most of the oil, independence would have to be negotiated, and essential UK interests would be involved. Moreover, the UK Government now has "joint participation" with the oil companies in the development of the oilfields, and any independence settlement would have to involve a guarantee by Scotland to provide a "fair return" to the rest of the UK in recognition of its capital stake. For these reasons, the Scottish Government would do well to receive two-thirds of the oil revenues, and this is what is assumed here.

Monetary union: While there would be pressures to maintain the monetary union, so that it might survive Scottish independence, it is more likely that the constraints that this would involve on the freedom of action of a newly independent government would be unacceptable to it. It is more reasonable to suppose that Scotland would leave the monetary union, establish its own monetary system and allow the Scots £ to vary in relation to the UK £.

On this basis, it is possible to trace out the major effects of independence on Scotland's economy.

Balance of payments: If the Scottish Government left the rate of depletion unchanged, it would receive £2,000 million a year in oil revenues and the balance of payments would benefit accordingly. The Government would, however, be under pressure to cut the depletion rate both to conserve the oil, and for environmental reasons. On the other hand, it would be under pressure to deliver many of the benefits which had been promised, and it would have the oil companies to contend with. It is unlikely therefore that the depletion rate would be halved, as has been suggested in some quarters. A much more modest cut might be made, say 10 to 15 per cent — which would reduce revenues by £400 million per year, leaving an annual flow of £1,600 million.

This figure, however, would not represent the balance of payments surplus; this would be reduced by Scotland's existing "non-oil" deficit. According to the best estimates we have, this has been running at about 10 per cent of Scotland's GDP for some time, which makes it now about £600 million. So Scotland's initial balance of payments surplus following independence might be of the order of £1,000 million, or about 15 per cent of Scotland's GDP.

Rate of inflation: It is unlikely that the payments surplus could be maintained for long, and very likely that Scotland's rate of inflation would begin to rise. On the demand side, while it is not inevitable that the new oil money would cause excess demand to appear, it seems reasonable to suppose that, following independence which had come about because the Scottish people wanted to cash in on an oil bonanza, there would be enormous pressures both for increases in public expenditure and for tax reductions.

The Government might in any case favour the creation of excess demand to raise the rates of employment and growth, and in this case, the inflationary pressures would not be resisted. On the cost side, a huge spate of wage demands could be expected, as different groups in society determined to seize "their share" of the new wealth they had been told independence would bring.

As the price level in Scotland rose, for both demand and cost reasons, and as rising consumer demand caused the rate of importing to increase steadily, the balance of payments surplus would steadily disappear; in effect, the income from oil, at first accruing only to the Government, would be translated into a higher standard of living throughout the country, by the mechanism of social conflict. The gain in income per head, on the basis of the analysis so far, would be about 15 per cent.

Exchange rate: With an initial large balance of payments surplus, the Scottish Government would be unable to prevent the exchange rate rising. It would see advantage in this in helping to control the rate of inflation, but the damage a rising rate or "strong pound" would do to the competitiveness of Scottish industry would also be evident. The Government would therefore wish to restrict the rise in the rate, and would do this by arranging for or permitting the export of capital — i.e. investing oil revenues overseas — and this would further reduce the overall balance of payments surplus.

In so far as oil revenues were invested abroad, they would, of course, not be available to raise incomes in Scotland: the figure to have in mind as an indicator of the likely gain in incomes per head as a result of independence is therefore much less than 15 per cent.

Employment: It is fair to anticipate a rising level of internal demand following independence, both because of the inflationary pressure and because of deliberate Government policy. This would be helpful for business and employment. But most of Scottish industry does not serve the Scottish market. Most Scottish goods are sold in the English market and overseas. Following Scottish independence, the rest of the UK would be depressed and demand for Scottish goods there would be low. Moreover, the position of Scottish industry in English markets would never wholly recover as the UK £ floated down and the Scots £ floated up.

As for overseas markets, as the Scots pound floated up (augmented by the rising inflation rate), Scottish industry would continue to lose competitiveness, and its existing rate of decline would be speeded up. Thus following independence there would soon develop a chronic problem of structural unemployment, not amenable to Keynesian measures because of the openness of the Scottish economy. The rate of job losses might easily rise to 35,000 a year, at which rate it would only take three years for unemployment in Scotland to rise to 10 per cent.

Investment and growth: Some of the supporters of separatism argue that a Scottish Government with access to oil revenues would be able to "regenerate" the Scottish economy, so that there would be dynamic gains to add to the once-over gain in income per head which has already been mentioned. It is important to consider of what order such "dynamic gains" might be.

The Scottish Government might seek to raise the rate of investment by increasing the level of internal demand and raising the rates of assistance to industry at present given under the regional policy. The limited effect of raising the level of demand in the Scottish economy has already been explained. As for attracting new industry by raising rates of assistance, the rising exchange rate would make Scotland an unattractive location for mobile industry serving markets in England or the EEC, and assistance would have to be increased substantially simply to maintain the present position.

If, nevertheless, it is conceded that these measures might have some effect in raising the rate of investment, it remains true that according to the best evidence we have, the rate of investment has to be raised a great deal (say 50 per cent) in order to raise the growth rate a little (say 1 per cent). It is rational to suppose therefore that any increase in Scotland's growth rate following independence would be very small.

So the overall conclusion which emerges from an analysis of the economic benefits and costs of independence is two-fold. On the one hand, there might be an increase in income per head of "less than 15 per cent", depending on the extent to which oil revenues were invested abroad. It might be best to take more explicit account of this factor and think in terms of a gain between 5 per cent and 10 per cent.

On the other hand, considerable costs would be incurred, including damage to Scotland's industrial structure as the rate of decline of Scottish industry speeded up; large-scale structural unemployment; serious inflationary pressure damaging not only Scotland's economy but also the cohesion of its society.

Whatever balance the partisans on different sides of the argument might choose to strike between these gains and costs, it is certainly not obvious that the Scottish people should regard independence as desirable from the economic point of view, however they regard it on other grounds.

And there is another factor in the background — the risk of economic disaster to an economy dependent for its viability on oil revenues, should the price of oil drift down.

If the independence game really is not worth the economic candle, it should be recognised that it is not, if only so that people can make a fair assessment of the relative benefits contained in the devolution proposals, If independence, because of the costs and risks involved, is not on balance preferable to the present situation, and if devolution offers Scotland economic benefits, then it will be devolution and not separatism which is Scotland's best economic option.

A Rejoinder D.I.Mackay

Major constitutional questions such as devolution, federalism or independence cannot be resolved on narrow economic arguments. Hence, it is not my purpose here to advocate any type of constitutional settlement for Scotland for the following analysis is concerned solely with the comparative economic advantages conferred on Scotland by (a) devolution as currently proposed, and (b) independence.

Christopher Smallwood has suggested that the economic benefits conferred on Scotland by the former are greater than, or at least comparable to, the economic benefits arising from independence. In particular he suggests that the economic benefits arising from North Sea oil and gas production are much less than is commonly supposed. I find his argument quite unconvincing as it rests on the fundamental premise that the Scots would choose an economic policy of almost criminal recklessness. Governments do sometimes act in this way as British citizens know to their cost. However, it is of little interest to argue that misconceived policies will dissipate any advantage. We can all accept that proposition. Of more interest, or at least of more interest to the dispassionate observer, is whether devolution or independence provides a better framework within which to apply **sensible** economic policy to deal with Scotland's economic problems.

It might be useful to begin by stating the area of agreement between Christopher Smallwood and myself. I would accept the following points he raises:

(1) He estimates that **on present policies** there might be an annual revenue from oil production of some £3,000 million annually by the 1980s.

(2) In the event of Scottish independence some part of oil revenues is likely to accrue to England and Wales. However, it appears probable that the bulk of the revenues would accrue to Scotland and Smallwood assumes that Scotland's share might amount to two-thirds of the total.

(3) Revenue on this scale would result in a massive surplus on the current account of Scotland's balance of payments.

(4) Given the situation described in (1) and (3) the exchange rate would tend to float upwards, making it more difficult for the traditional exporting industries to compete in world markets unless their efficiency could be improved. This process cannot be accomplished easily and an attempt to force the pace would both increase the rate of inflation and the level of unemployment.

All this seems to be quite incontestable. However, the final outcome Smallwood predicts will only arise **given** the inappropriate policies which he suggests. They do not represent the inevitable outcome of independence. More sensible policies offer the prospect of real economic advantage and we should pursue this rather than the hares let out of the bag by Christopher Smallwood.

First , it is clear that the reserves of North Sea oil and gas are so large that they would remove, for an extremely long period, any constraint on Scottish economic growth arising from an unfavourable balance of payments current account. There is no need at all to allow this to be reflected immediately in a rise in the exchange rate. Smallwood arrives at this conclusion by making an implicit assumption that a Scottish government would follow the same rate of depletion as a British government. This is an extraordinary position to adopt as it implies that a policy suitable for an economy with a population of 55 million is also suitable for an economy one-tenth of that size. Of course, it is not and it should hardly surprise us to find that Smallwood can "prove" such a policy unsuitable. Once this assumption falls the whole of Smallwood's argument collapses, and the assumption must fall for the rate of depletion of oil and gas reserves is not established by divine authority. If a quick rate of depletion yields too large a surplus on current account then the rate of depletion can always be reduced. There is little room to doubt that an independent Scottish government would choose a much lower rate of depletion than that likely to be chosen by a British government. All that we are saying is that as the balance of payments problems of Scotland and Britain would be different, the depletion policies which would be appropriate are also different (compare Norwegian and U.K. depletion policies) .

Again, Smallwood pays little attention to the capital account of the balance of payments. A surplus on the current account can be offset by investment abroad. Smallwood argues that, "In so far as oil revenues are
103

invested abroad, they would of course not be available to raise incomes in Scotland". This is an extremely shortsighted view. Investment overseas produces a stream of **future** income which does raise national income. Those familiar with British economic history will understand the process and also the economic benefits it can confer. The use of oil revenues to finance capital investment abroad yielding a future income is one obvious means of spreading the benefits over a longer period. This could secure a favourable balance of payments position for a long period after the oil and gas reserves are exhausted.

In brief, North Sea oil and gas reserves offer the real possibility of "buying time" during which the fundamental restructuring of the Scottish economy can be attempted. The period of time bought can be extended by appropriate economic policies. Of course, it will be extremely difficult to deal with the underlying economic problem for Scotland, like Britain, is an extremely inefficient economy by the standards of Western Europe. Heavy and selective emigration has left Scotland very short of business and entrepreneurial skills, a shortage aggravated by the prevailing emphasis on other skills and professions. Decades of low investment, low labour productivity, restricted labour mobility and abysmal industrial relations are not changed by the acquisition of political independence. However, these difficulties must be faced in any constitutional environment; they are as much a present fact for devolution as for independence.

The crucial fact to grasp about North Sea oil and gas is that the major benefits accrue to central government which has the right to tax North Sea oil and gas production. Smallwood concedes that these benefits would arise to a Scotland with political independence. Certainly they will not accrue within the devolutionary framework currently proposed as this specifically excludes any revenue sharing scheme. Economic growth in an independent Scotland need not be restricted by balance of payments constraints. If one favours a "market approach", as I do, it would be perfectly possible to encourage investment by reducing corporation tax and to reduce the penal rate of taxation, which in present-day Britain inhibits risk-taking and the acquisition of skills. Smallwood appears to think that such measures would make little appreciable difference. For example, he suggests a 50 per cent increase in the rate of investment would raise the growth rate by 1 per cent, which he regards as very small. This appears to be a matter of arithmetic. A 1 per cent increase in the rate of economic growth represents, over any substantial period, a major difference in outcome. If Britain's growth rate over the last three decades had been 1 per cent higher, then it would compare favourably with other advanced industrial countries and we would all be a lot richer. Any reader who is not convinced should consult the compound interest formula and calculate the difference between, say 2 per cent and 3 per cent growth.

In short, independence and North Sea oil do not offer any easy solution to the real economic difficulties involved in restructuring the Scottish economy. It only offers a framework within which there is a good chance that sensible policies might find solutions. There are other constitutional possibilities, but here it must be said that Smallwood is strangely silent on the economic advantages which will accrue from the present devolutionary proposals. Perhaps this is not surprising as the proposals do not change fundamental economic relationships and will grant to a Scottish Assembly less power to raise its own revenue than that normally accorded to a local authority.

POSTSCRIPT TO THE DEBATE

C. R. Smallwood

Having read Professor MacKay's riposte to my article, I think it can fairly be said that he and I are in broad agreement about the likely economic consequences of independence for Scotland, and that the remaining differences between us are matters of political judgment rather than economic analysis. Perhaps I could illustrate this by making three points.

(1) In my article, I explained that a flood of new oil money into the Scottish economy would cause considerable disruption, and I suggested that anyone wishing to decide whether or not independence was desirable in economic terms would need to weigh the costs of such disruption against the gains in income per head which the oil money would also provide. I quite agree with Professor MacKay that my analysis rested on the assumption that a Scottish government would follow the same rate of depletion as a British government. The reason I assumed this is that it is indeed the policy of the Scottish National Party to maintain a depletion rate in excess of 100m. tons a year, and the purpose of the article was to trace out the economic effects of that policy. If, however, the policy were to be changed, and the new Scottish government were to cut down the depletion rate significantly, or were to invest oil revenues abroad on a large scale, then Professor MacKay and I agree that most of the disruption about which I wrote could be avoided. The corollary of this, however, is that the increase in Scottish national income would be correspondingly less, and would not be such as to justify the economic expectations which the political campaign in Scotland has generated. Too much emphasis should not be put on any particular set of figures, but if for the sake of argument Scotland did receive two-thirds of the oil revenues as I assumed in my article, and if the Scottish government say halved the depletion rate of the reserves it controlled, then after the existing Scottish trade deficit had been financed, the resulting increase in Scotland's national income might be of the order of £400 million to £500 million (1974 prices). This is the equivalent of 7 to 8 per cent of Scotland's GNP, and therefore fails to qualify as the expected bonanza.

(2) I agree with Professor MacKay that this would nevertheless be a gain worth having, and would buy a certain amount of time for restructuring the Scottish economy. But I am more sceptical than he is that the new money would in fact be used for this purpose. It seems to me that in the circumstances of newly won independence, political pressures and

105

expectations would be such as to cause what new funds there were to be diverted to meet many demands other than that for new industrial investment, so that the new opportunity to restructure Scottish industry would be much more limited than he supposes. But this is a political rather than an economic judgment, and therefore one on which we are entitled to differ.

(3) Where I disagree with Donald MacKay is in his assumption that devolution will not bring any economic advantages to Scotland. Again, the difference between us is one of political rather than economic judgment. My view is that, following devolution, more and more UK resources will be diverted to Scotland. The devolved services and now the Scottish Development Agency are to be financed from a block grant which the Scottish Assembly is to negotiate each year with the UK government. In these negotiations — and especially while the separatist party is enjoying electoral success — the Scottish Assembly will be in a bargaining position of considerable strength, so that it is not fanciful to suppose that the level of expenditure in Scotland, both on the social services and on industrial development, could be pushed up over a number of years by some hundreds of millions of pounds. This, after all, is the great fear of English MPs, and the principal reason why their support for the Devolution Bill may be difficult to secure.

My overall judgment, therefore, which I stress is a political one as much as it is economic, is that the financial and economic gains to Scotland
(i) of independence — assuming now that a "responsible" economic policy is adopted by the Scottish government, involving either a substantial reduction in the rate of depletion of the oil reserves, or heavy investment of the oil revenues abroad, to avoid the difficulties highlighted in my article; and
(ii) of devolution — assuming the block grant system works to Scotland's advantage in the way it seems likely to;
may well be broadly comparable.

ANOTHER POSTSCRIPT

D. I. MacKay

Christopher Smallwood and I may be close to agreement on a number of points, but the differences remain important. We agree that massive oil revenues could be used to sharply raise consumption in an independent Scotland but that, given the limited absorptive capacity of the Scottish economy, this would adversely affect the long-term competitive position of the economy. Again, we agree that raising the level of efficiency of the economy cannot be easily accomplished. Further, we could agree that neither the current devolutionary proposals, nor independence would suddenly and permanently produce a transformation of Scottish living standards. However, I do not believe that the current devolutionary proposals offer **any** real prospect of such a transformation, even in the long

106

run. On the other hand, oil revenues, by providing an extremely strong balance of payments position, could allow an independent Scotland to pursue policies which would have a good chance of producing significant long-run economic advantages. Of course there are other constitutional possibilities, but I believe any settlement which does not provide Scotland with some share of oil revenues, and the power to use them effectively, will not create the necessary conditions for a major improvement in economic performance. If a Scottish Assembly or Parliament does not obtain access to oil revenues then the major benefits of North Sea oil will pass Scotland by. This proposition appears to be quite irrefutable and it is difficult to believe that such a situation will prove to be politically stable.

reference section

Bibliography

CH Allen

The lists below cover material published in the period 1.5.75 to 30.4.76, on Scottish politics, government, and policy issues (broadly interpreted). It is incomplete, not by intention but through lack of time; the largest gaps are in memoranda on the White Paper, **Our Changing Democracy** (of which at least a gross have been submitted, though few published), and in local government publications. Since the bibliography is envisaged as a regular feature of the **Yearbook,** any omissions will be included in next year's listing

The listing is divided into two parts, the first covering books. pamphlets, articles, memoranda, and longer newspaper features; the second includes shorter articles and newspaper features. There is a break in the numbering of the two sections (II begins at 200), to allow for easier identification of longer pieces in the Index, which is at the end of the lists.

Because of their frequent appearance, certain periodical and newspaper titles have been reduced to initials, thus:

APJ	Press and Journal (Aberdeen)
G	Guardian
GH	Glasgow Herald
Q	Question
S	Scotsman
SI	Scottish Independent
ST	Sunday Times
T	Times
TESS	Times Educational Supplement (Scotland)
WHFP	West Highland Free Press
WS	Weekend Scotsman

For UK newspapers, the relevant edition is that distributed in Edinburgh

PART 1: **Books, pamphlets and longer articles**

1 Aberdeen People's Press **Oil over Troubled Waters.** Aberdeen,, 1976,55pp
2 Adams, G "The Highlands' dilemma", **New Society,** 26.2.76, 436 7
3 Alexander, K "A new Scottish political economy", **Scottish Review,** 1, 1 (1975), 12-15
4 Alexander, K **Change and opportunity in Scotland today,** Glasgow, 1976

4a Alexander, K W J "The Political economy of change", pp 109-25 of **The Political Economy of Change,** ed Alexander (Oxford, 1975)
5 Anon. "Devolution proposals to be recast feeling in Lords", **County Councils Gazette,** 68, 12 (1976), 317-21
6 Anon. "The future of the profession", **Journal of the Law Society of Scotland,** 20, 5 (1975), 160-78 and 20, 7 (1975), 246-8
7 Anon. "The great 4-day debate on devolution", **County Councils Gazette,** 68,11 (1976), 295-300
8 Association of University Teachers (Scotland): **The Scottish universities under Government devolution.** Glasgow, 1976, 2pp
9 Association of University Teachers (Scotland): **The Scottish universities and devolution; safeguarding of academic freedom.** Glasgow, 1976
10 Begg, H; Lythe, C; Sorley, R **Expenditure in Scotland, 1961-71.** Edinburgh: Scottish Academic Press, 1975
11 Bell, D "Regional unemployment in Scotland", **Quarterly Economic Bulletin** (Fraser of Allender Institute), 1,2 (1975), 21-28 plus tables
12 Blue, A **The Sound of Sense.** Glasgow: the Author, 1975, 47+iv pp
13 Bochel, J M & Denver, D G **The Scottish Local Government Elections 1974.** Edinburgh: Scottish Academic Press, 1975, 176pp
14 Boyce D G "Dicey, Kilbrandon and devolution", **Political Quarterly,** 46,3 (1975), 280-92
15 Breeze, P "Oil and Scotland: a review of current developments", **Scottish Marxist** 11 (1976), 28-34
16 British Medical Association: "Devolution to Scotland and Wales", **British Medical Journal,** 20.3.76, 724-7
17 British Medical Association (Scottish Council): **Memorandum on 'Our Changing Democracy'.** Edinburgh, 1976, 4pp

18   Brown, G (Ed.) **The Red Paper on Scotland.** Edinburgh: Student Publication Board, 1975, 368pp

19   Burnett, R; McEwen, J "The Argyll islands", **Calgacus** 2 (1975), 22-8, 40-41

20   Calvert, H **Devolution.** London: Professional Books, 1975, 201 pp

21   Central Office of Information: **Devolution. The new Assemblies for Scotland and Wales.** London: HMSO, 1976, 15pp

22   Christie, D J "Our changing democracy", **Scots Law Times,** 5.3.76, 65-70

23   Clarke, M G "The Assembly and local government", **New Edinburgh Review,** 31 (1976), 37-42

24   Cochrane, H et al. "The faceless men who really run Scotland", **GH,** 6-9.10.75

25   Commission of the European Communities: **Scotland and Europe.** Edinburgh, 1975, 29pp

26   Confederation of British Industries (Scotland): **Memorandum on the White Paper 'Our Changing Democracy'.** Glasgow, 1976

27   Convention of Scottish Local Authorities: **Memorandum of observations** (on Cmnd 6348). Edinburgh, 1976, 25pp

28   Czerkawska, C L **Fisherfolk of Carrick.** Glasgow: Molendinar Press, 1975

29   Davidson, I "The nuclear threat to Scotland", **Scottish Marxist** 10 (1975), 31-36

30   Day, M "Environmental improvement in Glasgow", **Town and Country Planning** 43 (June 1975), 317-20

31   Donnachie, I **The Open University and Scottish Devolution: some points for discussion.** Edinburgh: Open University, 1976, 6pp

32   Drucker, H "A pedigree for the White Paper", **New Edinburgh Review** 31 (1976), 2-8

33   Easton, N "The development of Scottish nationalism" (12 parts). **Scottish Worker,** 2,1 (1975) to 3,3 (1976)

34   Edinburgh Association of University Teachers: **Statement on the White Paper on Devolution.** Edinburgh, 1976, 3pp

35   Elliott, B & McCrone, D "Landlords in Edinburgh: some preliminary observations". **Sociological Review,** 23,3 (1975), 539-62

36   Faculty of Advocates: **Memorandum on the White Paper on devolution:** Edinburgh, 1976, 33pp

37   Firn, J **External Control and regional development: the case of Scotland.** Glasgow University, Urban and Regional Studies, Discussion Paper 16, 1976, 28pp

38   French, S "Simon French meets the Directors" (of Education), **Scottish Educational Journal,** 58, 26-38 (1975), 753-4, 781, 806-7, 829, 860-1, 886-7, 915, 941, 968, 989, 1009, 1035

39   Fry, M et al. "Scotland and the world economy", S, 20-24.10.75

40   Gilmour, J **Electing the Scottish Assembly.** London: Electoral Reform Society, 1975, 36pp

41   Gollan, J "Scotland today", **Scottish Marxist,** 10 (1975), 37-41 (Review of **The Red Paper on Scotland,** ed. G Brown)

42   Gunn, L A "The Assembly and its servants", **New Edinburgh Review** 31 (1975), 42-46

43   Harrison, A **The distribution of personal wealth in Scotland.** Glasgow: Fraser of Allender Institute, Monograph 1, 1975

45   Heald, D **Making devolution work.** London: Young Fabian Pamphlet 43, 1976, 56pp

46   Heald, D "Financing devolution", **National Westminster Bank Quarterly Review,** November 1975, 6-16

47   Hechter, M **Internal Colonialism: the Celtic fringe in British national development 1536-1966** London: Routledge, Kegan Paul, 1975, 361pp. Reviews by D. Harrison in **Scottish Marxist** 11 (1976), 42-48 and O. D. Edwards in **Scottish Independent** 60 (1976), 9-10.

48   Henissart, P "Scotland's future: the British question" **Readers Digest** Jan 1976 27-32

49   Hughes, J "Industrial development" (and devolution), **New Edinburgh Review** 31 (1976), 29-35

50   Jacobs, S "Community action in a Glasgow clearance area: consensus or conflict", in P. Leonard (ed), **The Sociology of Community Action.** London: Sociological Review Monograph 21, 1975

51   Jones, M "The oil rush", **New Statesman,** 23.1-13.2.76

52   Judge, D & Finlayson, D A "Scottish MPs and devolution", **Parliamentary Affairs,** 28,3 (1975), 278-92

53   Kellas, J C **The Scottish Political System,** 2nd edition. Cambridge: Cambridge University Press, 1975, 250pp

54   Kellas, J C **Devolution in British politics.** Paper to the Political Science Association Conference, Nottingham, March 1976

55   Kellas, J C "Administering Scotland: a critique and forward look", pp162-70 of **The Political Economy of Change,** ed. K W J Alexander (Oxford 1975)

55a Kellas, J C "Oil, federalism and devolution", **Round Table** 259 (1975), 273-80

56   Kellas, J C **The application of federalism to the UK.** Louvain: European Consortium for Political Research, 1976

57   Kennedy, G **A defence policy for Scotland.** Edinburgh: Fletcher Paper 1, 1976, 41pp

58   Kennedy, G "Scotland and Europe", **New Europe,** Jan 1976

59   Kiernan, V "A Scottish road to socialism?", **New Left Review** 93 (1975), 93-104

60   Kinnear, W J "Scotland: the Middle East of Europe?", **Scottish Bankers Magazine,** 66,267 (1975), 183-90

61   Labour Party (Scottish Council): **Analysis of the economics of separation.** Glasgow, 1976

62 Lamont, A **How Scots opposed the peacetime call-up.** Carlops: Scots Secretariat, 1976. 31pp

63 Lord Hunter "Scots law. The legislative machine", **Scots Law Times,** 1975, 121-9

64 McAllister, R A "A White Paper with few friends", **New Edinburgh Review** 31 (1976), 46-52

65 McCluskey, J H "The social responsibility of the lawyer" (extracts), **Scolag Bulletin** 3 (1976), 19-23

66 MacColla, F **Too long in this condition.** Caithness: John Humphries, 1975, 112pp

67 MacCormick, I (MP) "The Assembly and UK Departments", **New Edinburgh Review** 31 (1976), 17-21

68 MacCormick, N **Independence and federalism after the referendum.** Edinburgh: Fletcher Paper 4, 1976, 9pp

69 Mackay, D I "North Sea oil and the Scottish economy", pp 126-50 of **The Political Economy of Change,** ed. K W J Alexander (Oxford 1975)

69a Mackay, D I **North Sea oil through speculative glasses.** Glasgow: Fraser of Allander Institute, 1975

70 Mackay, D I & G A **The Political Economy of North Sea Oil.** London: Martin Robertson, 1975, 193pp

71 McKay, I "The devolution issue" **Scottish Marxist** 11 (1076). 18-23

72 Mackay, R "Protestant extremists in Scotland", **Calgacus** 2 (1975), 7-10

73 Mackintosh, J P (MP) "The power of the Secretary of State". **New Edinburgh Review** 31 (1976) 9-16

74 Mackintosh, J P (MP) **A parliament for Scotland.** Tranent: Berwick and East Lothian Constituency Labour Party, 1975, 22pp

75 McNicoll, I H **The Shetland economy.** Glasgow: Fraser of Allander Institute, Research Monograph 2, 1976

76 McPherson, A F "National differences in pedagogy and first year achievement at Edinburgh University", **Scottish Educational Studies,** 7,2 (1975), 49-66

77 MacRae, T **North Sea oil and the Scottish economy.** Edinburgh: Fletcher Paper 2, 1976, 39pp

78 Miller, W **Four-way swing in Scotland 1955-74: pathmakers in British politics.** Scottish/Norwegian conference, 1975

79 Myers, P "The Commissioner for Local Administration", **Scots Law Times,** 24.10.75, 229-32

80 National Union of Students (Scotland): **Response ... to the Government's White Paper: 'Our Changing Democracy'.** Edinburgh 1976, 7pp

80a Oakley, C A et al. "Does Glasgow flourish?" **Life and Work,** March 1976, 15-26

81 Parvin, G & Smith, P **Scotland's voice in Europe.** Edinburgh: Scottish Conservative Policy Forum, 1976

82 Privy Council **Our Changing Democracy: devolution to Scotland and Wales.** London: HMSO (Cmnd 6348), 1975, 73pp

83   Reid, H "The secondary (schools) sickness", **S**, 22-25.3.76
84   Reid, J "Interview", **Masque** (Glasgow), April 1976, 11-15
84a Rose, R **The future of Scottish politics: a dynamic analysis.** Glasgow: Fraser of Allander Institute, 1975, 26pp
85   Ross, J "Local government reorganisation: Glasgow's future", **Scottish Marxist 9** (1975), 28-35
86   Rowe, A **Democracy Renewed.** London: Sheldon Press, 1975, 119pp
87   Royal College of Physicians of Edinburgh: **White Paper on Devolution.** Edinburgh, 1976, 2pp
88   **Scotsman. State of the nation.** Edinburgh, 19.1.76, 8pp, and 26.1.76, 8pp (supplements to the **Scotsman**)
89   **Scotsman.** "Tomorrow's Scots", S, 26-29.4.76 (opinion survey)
90   Scott, J & Hughes, M "Ownership and control in a satellite economy: a discussion from Scottish data", **Sociology, 10, 1** (1976), 21-42
91   Scottish Conservative Central Office: **Devolution brief.** Edinburgh, 1975, 8pp
92   Scottish Conservative Devolution Committee: **Statement** (on future Scottish representation at Westminster). London: House of Commons, 3.11.75, 5pp
93   Scottish Conservative Devolution Committee: **Statement** (on taxation and revenue powers of the Assembly), Edinburgh: Conservative Central Office, 30.9.75, 4pp
94   Scottish Conservative Devolution Committee: **Statement** (on the Assembly and the structure of local government), Edinburgh: Conservative Central Office, 13.10.75, 3pp
95   Scottish Conservative Devolution Committee: **Statement** (on the method of election and the electoral system for the Assembly), Edinburgh: Conservative Central Office 22.9.75, 6pp
96   Scottish Conservative Devolution Committee: **Statement** (on the type of Assembly and its links with Westminster). Edinburgh: Conservative Central Office, 5.1.76, 3pp
97   Scottish Conservative Devolution Committee: **Statement with regard to the Government White Paper on devolution.** Edinburgh: Conservative Central Office, 5.1.76, 3pp
98   Scottish Labour Party: **Sentinel.** Glasgow, 1975, 20pp
98a Scottish Labour Party: **Jobs and Industry,** Glasgow, 1976
99   Scottish Liberal Party: **Resolutions passed at the 1975 conference at Ayr.** Edinburgh, 1975, 6pp

100 Scottish Liberal Party: **Evidence on the White Paper Cmnd 6348.** Edinburgh, 1976, 4pp plus appendices
101a **Scottish Miner** "Common Market special", **Scottish Miner,** May 1975
101 Scottish National Party: **Scotland's oil: the background.** Edinburgh SNP Research Department, 1975, 7pp
102 Scottish National Party: **A partnership in health care.** Edinburgh: SNP Health Policy Committee, 1975, 711
104 Scottish National Party: **Comments on Cmnd. 6348: 'Our Changing**

Democracy ' Edinburgh, 1976, 5pp
105 Scottish Office **The benefits of North Sea Oil.** Edinburgh, 1976
106 Scottish Office **Developments in land use planning in Scotland.**
Edinburgh: Scottish Information Office Reference Unit, 1975, 13pp
107 Scottish Office **Secretary of State's responsibility for industry in**
Scotland. Edinburgh: Scottish Information Office Reference Unit,
1975, 4pp
108 Scottish Secondary Teachers Association: **Observations on the White**
Paper on devolution to Scotland and Wales. Edinburgh, 1976, 3pp
109 Scottish Universities Devolution Action Committee: **Devolution of the**
universities (Address to the Lord President of Council). Edinburgh,
1976, 3pp
110 Sillars, J (MP) Interview, **Masque** (Glasgow), April 1976, 37-9
110a Simpson, D "Economic growth in Scotland: theory and experience",
pp. 151-61 of **The Political Economy of Change,** ed. K. W J Alexander
(Oxford, 1975)
111 Slesser, M **Scotland and Energy.** Edinburgh: Fletcher Paper 3, 1976,
19pp
112 Smallwood, C "Financing the Assembly", **New Edinburgh Review** 31
(1976), 22-28

113 Smith, P "The crisis, Scotland the Common Market", **Scottish**
Marxist 9 (1975), 8-14
114 Stacey, F **British Government 1966-75.** London: Oxford University
Press, 1975, 243pp. See pp 144-56, on regional devolution.
115 Stout, C H **Financial proposals in the White Paper.** Edinburgh:
District Council, 1975, 16pp
116 Sutherland, R "Devolution: the bond of sovereignty", **Journal of the**
Law Society of Scotland, 20,9 (1975), 312-17
117 Sutherland, R "Devolution the accessories of sovereignty", **Journal**
of the Law Society of Scotland 20, 11 (1975), 382-5
118 Swan, I "International Women's Year", **Scottish Marxist** 9 (1975),
23-26
119 System Three **Attitudes to finance and organisation of public**
transport. Dundee, 1976, 611 plus appendices
120 Tait, A A **The economics of devolution - a knife-edge problem.**
Glasgow: Fraser of Allander Institute, 1975. 12pp
121 Tait, B "Socialist education: what kind of qualification is that?",
Masque (Glasgow), April 1976, 33-36
122 Tait, J "The lessons of Kingston Halls", **Scottish Marxist** 10 (1975),
24-30
123 Thomson, G "Scotland and the EEC", **Scottish Bankers Magazine,**
22,266 (1975), 98-104
124 Webb, K & Hall, E **Explanations of political nationalism in Scotland.**
Louvain: European Consortium on Political Research Workshop on
Political Behaviour, Dissatisfaction and Protest, 1976, 60pp
125 Willock, I D "The Scottish Law Commission", **Scolag Bulletin** 2 (1975),
37-40

126 Wilson, A **The Sound of Silence: subsidy and competition in West Coast shipping.** Glasgow: the author, 1975, 77pp
127 Wilson, A **The Sound of the Clam.** Glasgow: the author, 1975, 79pp
128 Wyn Ellis, N "A voice from the ranks" (Tam Dalyell), **Sunday Times Magazine,** 12.10.75, 75-84

Part 2: Short articles and features

201 'Albannach' "A Scottish oil worker's view of life on the North Sea", **SI** 56 (1975, 5
202 Alexander, K W J Interview (with Brian Barr), **WHFP,** 24.10.75, 2
203 Allsopp, W "SDN: deadline tomorrow", **ST,** 26.10.75, 61
204 Anon. "A mismanaged Health Service", **Q** 1 (1975), 6-7
205 Anon. "Ayr farmers seek union probe", **Scottish Farmer,** 1.10.75, 15, 17
206 Anon. "Big, bad Sir John, and the Kishorn carve-up", **WHFP** 1.8.75, 1,3
207 Anon. "Coming, coming, came," **Q4** (1976), 6-7 (on SLP)
208 Anon. "Devolve and rule?", **Economist** 14.2.76 , 36-7
209 Anon. "Devolution and the law", **Scotlag Bulletin** 2 (1976), 26-7
210 Anon. "Devolution: keeping the politicians apart", **Economist** 7.2.76 , 25-6
211 Anon. "Devolution: Labour's plans for Scotland are inadequate", **Scottish Miner,** Dec. 1975, 3
212 Anon. "Devolution: sleeping in a minefield", **Economist** 15.11.75 , 34
213 Anon. "Give school councils real power says Moray House report" **TESS** 2.5.75, 18
214 Anon. "How to devolve?", **Spectator,** 6.12.75, 715 (and 721-2)
215 Anon. "If Scottish Labour fails it may be a Disunited Kingdom" **Economist,** 20.12.75, 17-18
216 Anon. "Lest the axe fall", **Economist,** 17.1.76, 12-14
217 Anon. "More referendums?", **Economist,** 6.1.76, 11-13
218 Anon. Opinion polls: devolution. **S,** 2-3.6.75; 16-18.12.75; **GH,** 17.11.75, 1,3
219 Anon. Opinion poll: EEC, **GH,** 12.5.75,1 and 2.6.75, 1
220 Anon. "Scotland's two nations", **Economist,** 10.1.76, 56-7
221 Anon. " SDN: what went wrong?", **WHFP,** 10,10.75, 2
222 Anon. "Slump's Scottish child", **Economist,** 1.11.75, 16-17
223 Anon. "Student s say SNP OK", **Free Student Press,** Spring 1976, 1
224 Anon. "The dangers of devolution", **Teeside Journal of Commerce,** Feb. 1976, 47
225 Anon. "The defence aims and needs of a free Scotland", **SI** 61 (1976) . 9
226 Anon. "The devolution fling", **Economist,** 29.11.75, 13-15
227 Anon. "The Scot's birse is up", **SI** 58 (1976), 1
228 Anon. "The Scottish Office answer their own questions (on crofting) ". **WHFP,** 19.12.75, 2-3
229 Anon. "The strategy for freedom",, **SI** 60 (1976), 1, 7

230   Anon. "Troon: the Labour Party Conference", **Q** 7 (1976), 2
231   Ascherson, N "A dead end in devolution feared",S,2.9.75, 11

232   Ascherson, N "A long drought but now the monsoon", S, 12.11.75, 13
233   Ascherson, N "Capital punishment for the Scottish entrepreneur", S, 16.3.76, 11
234   Ascherson, N "Deep thinking on the Assembly", S, 14.10.75, 14
235   Ascherson, N "Europe and the Celtic conundrum", **Observer,** 25.5.75, 10
236   Ascherson, N "If there is an SNP majority", S, 7.2.76, 6
237   Ascherson, N "Labour may U-turn through chink in Foot's mind", S, 20.4.76, 9
238   Ascherson, N "Labour MPs are rallied to devolution cause", S, 5.11.75, 11
239   Ascherson, N "Labour try to halt the rout", S, 25.3.76, 15
240   Ascherson, N "Left join the battle over croft land", **WS,** 31.1.76, 1
241   Ascherson, "Mr Johnston at the crossroads", S, 9.7.75, 11
242   Ascherson, N "New cures for the plague on Scotland's housing", S, 29.7.75, 9
243   Ascherson, N "No easy label for the SNP", S, 9.4.76
244   Ascherson, N "Post referendum prospect is reassuring," S, 28.5.75, 11
245   Ascherson, N "Return journey", **Q** 2 (1075), 4-5
246   Ascherson, N "Scotland's choice: autonomy or autocracy" S, 7.7.75, 6
247   Ascherson, N "Scotland's new 'Callaghan man' ", S, 16.4.76
248   Ascherson, N "Scotland's place in the world: Labour remain odd man out", S, 25.6.75, 10
249   Ascherson, N "Scotland's socialist schismatics", S, 27.2.76, 10
252   Ascherson, N "Taking a rise out of Nalgo", S, 25.7.75 (letter: 28.11.75)
253   Ascherson, N "The continental system", S, 9.9.75, 10
254   Ascherson,N "The metamorphosis of a moralising Marxist", S, 13.2.76, 11
255   Ascherson, N "The name of the game is devolution", **Scotsman Half Yearly Review** (Jan.-June 1975), 1
256   Ascherson, N "The veto's forbidding aspects", S, 22.10.75, 11
257   Ascherson, N "Thorpe thought's about devolution", S, 5.12.75, 13
258   Ascherson, N "What Wester Hailes thinks today . . .", S, 5.9.75, 13
259   Ascherson, N "Where will the SDA fit in?" S, 28.7.75, 6
260   Ascherson, N "Wilson's double gamble on devolution", S, 22.11.75
261   Ashley, R "The SDN story", **Spectator,** 11.10.75, 481-2
262   Associations of County Councils: "Why the ACC reject the White Paper proposals on devolution", **County Council Gazette,** 68,11 (1976), 293-4
263   Association of County Councils: "Devolution: the possible dangers", **County Councils Gazette,** 68,10 (1976), 262-3
264   Baggott, M "Europe's new interest", **Scotsman Half Yearly Review** (Jan.-June 1975), 3
265   Baggott, M "Scotland less slow on the upturn", S, 29.4.76
266   Baggott, M "SDA, the Scottish Development Acorn", S, 16.12.75, 11

267 Baggott, M "STUC leader steps down", **S**, 11.12.75
268 Baggott, M "Sir William Gray to head SDA", **S**, 15.8.75, 9
269 Bain D "Hands of our currency", **SI**, 53 (1975), 4
270 Bain, M (MP) "Tactical 'no' by Scots" **Scottish Educational Journal**, 58, 21 (1975), 621
271 Bain, M (MP) "When a woman goes to Westminster", **Sunday Post**, 26.10.75, 9
272 Barr, B "Our Freedom Fighters", **WHFP**, 30.5.75, 2
273 Barr, D "Making the political jigsaw fit". A.P.J. 16.4.76, 10.
274 Bayne, I "Can the West be won", (by SNP) **Q**1 (1975), 13-14
275 Bayne, I 'Ideology and 7: 84' ,**Q3 (1975)**, 17-18; reply **Q4** (1976), 18-19
276 Beaumont, PB "Workforce on the move", **S**, 10.7.75, 10
277 Bell, C "The developing saga of Dean Village", **WS**, 17.4.76, 2
278 Bell, C "Dundee: a city on the road to nowhere", **WS**, 13.3.76, 1
279 Bell, C "Tam Dalyell: a blunt but pertinaceous instrument", **WS**, 15.11.75, 6
280 Bell, C "The state of the Liberals", **Q1**, (1975), 4-5
281 Bell, H "Thinking costs nothing", **Q4**, (1976), 4-5
282 Bell, R E "Subservient universities", **TESS**, 29.8.75, 11
283 Beveridge, L "Developer s'castles in the air", **S**, 27.4.76, 9
284 Bochel, D & Maclaren, M "Democracy and the health council", **S**, 17.5.75, 8
285 Bradford, D "Backbenchers' beliefs on devolution", **S**, 11.3.76, 11
286 Bradford, D "Finale for 'Basso Profundo'?" (W. Ross), **S**, 18.3.76, 13
287 Bradford, D "Pacing devolution progress is Labour's dilemma", **S**, 22.1.76, 11
288 Bradford, D "Wrath of Gael and gale of wrath" (W. Ross), **S**, 9.4.76, 13
289 Brand, J & McCrone, D "The SNP: from protest to nationalism", **New Society**, 20.11.75, 416-8
290 Breach, I "City Slickers" (Aberdeen) **G**, 28.10.75, 14
291 Brown, G "Labour's road back", **Q6** (1976), 11-12
292 Brown, G "Labour - where the strength lies", **Q4**, (1976), 11-12
293 Brown, H (MP) "Reply to 'The Crofter's Charter'," **WHFP**, 28.1.76, 6
294 Brown, R "Beware of the dinosaurs" (SLP & devolution), **GH**, 28.1.76, 6
295 Bruce, I "Dads Army and the North Sea rigs", **GH**, 26.8.75, 7
296 Buchan, N (MP) "Scenario for a Scottish referendum", **WHFP**, 2.4.76, 2
297 Buchan, N (MP) "Scots missed", **G**, 22.3.76
298 Buchan, N (MP) "Scottish devolution: why democracy demands a referendum", **T**, 4.11.75, 12
299 Buchan, N (MP) "Who's afraid of a referendum?", **WS**, 14.2.76, 6
300 Burnett, R "Board accountability should accompany tourist project", **WHFP**, 1.8.75, 2
301 Butt, R "Devolution: we walked the same road 50 years ago", **T**, 6.11.75,
302 Cain, A "After the power line enquiry", **WHFP**, 11.7.75, 2

303 Campbell, A "Shieldaig", **WHFP,** 20.2.76, 3
304 Campbell, J S "Planning appeals: public inquiry or written submission?", **Scots Law Times,** 20.2.76, 3
306 Carr, C "The SLP", **Scottish Worker,** 3,1 (1976), 3, 8
308 Chisholm, W "Speaker would give starting orders", S, 22.10.75, 11
309 'Cigaro', "The Bourbons of Keir Hardie House", **Q7,** (1976), 15-16
310 Clark, I "Shetland's lone stand on devolution", S, 14.11.75, 13
311 Clark, W "Is the devolution train back on the right lines?", **GH,** 18.3.76
312 Clark, W "Ross seeks Labour morale-booster after East Kilbride", **GH,** 5.2.76, 7
313 Clarke, W "Scotland's economic Culloden", **GH,** 29.12.75,7
314 Clarke, W "Shakeup in Scottish Tory office", **GH,** 12.5.75, 1
315 Clark, W "What now for Scotland's Tories after the doldrums of Dundee", **HG,** 19.5.75, 7 (letter: 22.5.75)
316 Clark Hutchison M (MP): "Scottish Assembly is 'Not inevitable'," **S,** 2.3.76, 10
317 Clark, Hutchison, M (MP): "Standing on our own feet", **S,** 3.6.75, 11 (letters: 9 & 13.6.75)
318 Cochrane, H "Eurocrats step in after Whitehall refuses grant", **GH,** 16.7.75, 7
319 Cochrane, H "Scotland's long, long wait for a decision on nuclear power", **GH,** 15.9.75, 7
320 Cochrane, H "Scotland: where so much is owned by so few", **GH,** 6.6.75, 7
321 Cochrane, H "Sir Andrew (Gilchrist) means to go out fighting",**GH,** 12.12.75
322 Cochrane, H "Taking on the oil giants: a no-nonsense Scotsman", (J. Smith), **GH,** 12.12.75, 7
323 Cochrane, H "The hot seat is just what the doctor ordered" (J Dickson Mabon), **GH,** 6.4.76, 7
325 Cochrane, H & MacBarnett, A "Onshore targets: an urgent matter of security", **GH,** 24.9.75, 7
326 Cochrane, H & MacCalman, J "Strathclyde: a bleak prospect", **GH,** 10.7.75,7
327 Cochrane, H et al. "Dossier on defence", **GH,** 26-27.5.75
328 Cook, R F (MP) "No room for separatism in Europe", S, 17.7.75, 2
329 Craigen, J (MP) "Scotland at Westminster", **Cooperative News,** 11.7.75,2
330 Crawford, D (MP) "Political dogma burdens SDA", S, 6.8.75, 2
331 Crawford, M "Could Scotland afford to stand alone?", **ST,** 30.11.75, 62
332 Cunningham, J "When tenants take on the council", **GH,** 1.4.76, 7
333 Currie, A "The SNP and participation", **Q7** (1976), 8-10
334 Dalyell T (MP) "Let's stop this Assembly now", **Evening News,** 24.11.75, 8
335 Davidson, J "A tale of three villages", **WS,** 7.6.75, 1
336 Davidson, J "Hebridean overtures", S, 4-6.12.75
337 Davidson, J "Now you see it - now you don't", S, 11.9.75, 11
338 Davidson, J "Why the North fears 'Scottish backlash', & "Motorway

to regional new deal", **S,** 20-21.2.76

339 Davie, M "What makes a Nat tick?", **Observer,** 1.2.76, 32

340 Deans, J "Millan is not over-fearful of SNP advance", **APJ,** 13.4.76, 8

341 Denholm, L "Devolution, education, democracy", **TESS,** 28.11.75, 4

342 Dickson, P "Drumbuie, Cramond and the underdog", **GH,** 13.6.75, 6

344 Donaldson, A "Very first impressions", **Q3** (1975), 5-6

345 Douglas-Home, C "Why 'back-door' devolution may be best", **T,** 28.2.76, 12

346 Drewry, G "Minor party MPs", **New Society.** 4.3.76. 494

346a Drucker, H M "Labour's ideological petard", **Q2** (1975), 8-9

346b Drucker, H M "Will politics wreck the Health Service in Scotland?", **Health and Social Service Journal,** 17.3.76, 587-9

347 Duckers, J "Where will the councils hand over land?", **APJ,** 23.4.76, 10

348 Duckworth, J "Assembly plan won't radically affect agriculture", **Scottish Farmer,** 6.12.75, 15

349 Duffy, K "Devolution and the press", **Q6,** (1976), 13

350 Dunn, P "This is 'Multiple urban deprivation'", **ST,** 15.6.75, 6

351 Easton, J "High noon at City Chambers", **GH,** 3.4.76, 7

352 Edwards, O D "Now you know", **Q6,** (1976), 7-8

353 Edwards, O D "This party that inspires a sense of real envy in others", **SI,** 52 (1975), 7

354 Edwards O D "Who's Sillars now?", **Q4** (1976), 2

355 Erickson, J "In defence of Scotland", **S,** 9.3.76, 10

356 Faux, R "Counting the cost of Scotland's new spendthrift councils", **T,** 28.8.75, 14

357 Faux, R "Scottish nationalists prepare for devolution", **T,** 24-28.10.75

358 Faux, R "The man from Quebec with a message for Scotland", **T,** 17.6.75, 14

360 Fay, S "How Nats would run Scotland - by the chief", **ST,** 16.11.75

361 Fenton, J "When the devolution comes", **News Statesmen,** 23.1.76, 86

362 Ferguson, B "Citizen Kane", **GH,** 10.3.76, 7

363 Findlay, A "Anatomy of the Scots Voter", **GH,** 19.1.76, 7 (see also p. 1)

364 Findlay, A "A seat in Europe for Scotland?", **GH,** 12.6.75, 6

365 Findlay, A "Bonn's lesson for London", **GH,** 21.4.76, 6

366 Findlay, A "From wildnerness to hot seat for Gray", **GH,** 15.8.75, 6

367 Firn, J "Divided responsibility weakens Assembly", **S,** 11.12.75, 12

368 Firth, H "Source of local finance vital", **S,** 3.7.75, 11

369 Firth, H "Whither Orkney and Shetland?", **Q6** (1976), 8-10

370 Fladmark, J M "Putting planning back on the rails", **S,** 13.4.76

371 Fletcher, A (MP) "A Scottish Assembly could point the way to more effective government throughout Britain", **T,** 12.8.75,12

372 Flockhart, R "In the councils of men", **Life & Work,** Dec. 1975, 31-2

373 Foulkes, G "In defence of local government", **S,** 8.9.75, 6

374 Foulkes, G "COSLA challenge to SED", **Scottish Educational Journal,** 59,5 (1976), 9-13

375 Frazer, F "Ammunition for economic separatist argument", **S,** 29.5.75, 11

377   Frazer, F "Flotta awaits the flood", **WS,** 3.1.76, 1
378   Frazer, F "The Islands of intransigentism", S 4.12.75, 13
379   Frazer, F; Mackay, D I & G A "Scotland downstream" S, 6-8.4.76
380   Fry, M "Assembly and the begging bowl," **S,** 4.2.76, 8
381   Fry, M "Constraints on the SDA", **S,** 29.10.75, 10
382   Fry, M "Country fit for the planners", **S,** 9.6.75, 6
383   Fry, M "Figures reveal padding of public payrolls", **S,** 10.2.76, 9
384   Fry, M "Robin Hood reversed", **S,** 16.12.75
385   Fry, M "Scotland's spending in the sixties", **S,** 15.5.75, 13
386   Fry, M "Purse strings pulled furth of Scotland", **S,** 28.5.75, 11
387   Fry, M "The not-so-poor are always with us", **S,** 31.7.75, 11
388   Fulton, T:Letter: selection of Assembly candidates, **S,** 31.7 75, 10
389   Gibson, P "Housing hiatus", **Q2** (1975), 12-14
390   Gibson, P "Housing with a human face", **Q3** (1975), 7-8
391   Gibson, P "How Assembly should support voluntary organisations", **S,** 10.4.76
392   Gilchrist, Sir A "Devolution and Scottish independence" (letter), **T,** 21.2.76
393   Gilchrist, Sir A "Retirement speech", **WHFP,** 21.11.75, 2
394   Gillies, C "Corruption: is this the tip of the iceberg", **GH,** 5.4.76, 7
395   Gillies, C "Free meals, cheap meals: but councillors are beginning to feel the pinch", **GH,** 30.1.76
396   Gillies, C "Legal aid: Scotland's solicitors attack the claims of fat profits", **GH,** 17.3.76, 7
397   Gillies, C "My £50 a week pay rise", **GH,** 17.7.75, 7
398   Gillies, C "What price cheap mortgages?",**GH,**22.8.75,6
399   Gilmour, J "The value of the vote", **Q1** (1975), 11-12
400   Glasgow Herald "Devolution: a Glasgow Herald guide", **GH,** 24.22.75, 7
401   Glasgow Herald "The great divide", **GH,** 4.6.75, 7
402   Glen, D "The Word is democracy", **Q3,** (1975), 16-17
403   Gordon, C "Build the SLP", **Scottish Worker,** 3,2 (1976), 1, 6
404   Gordon, C "Labour Party's 'devolution dilemma'", **Scottish Worker,** 2,6 (1975), 1, 8
405   Gordon, I "Community Councils: an alternative for the Western Isles", **WHFP,** 27.2.76, 2
.406   Gorrie, D "Civil servants and the 'nanny complex'", **WS,** 28.2.76, 2
407   Graham, T (MP) "Devolution", **Cooperative News,** 14.11.75, 2
408   Grant, J S Letter: owner occupany for crofters, **WHFP,** 26.8.75, 2
409   Grant, N "The nonsense remains", **Q3,** (1975), 11-12
410   Gray, I "Fighting to squash the stigma of squatting", **GH,** 8.9.75, 7
411   Grigor, I F "Landownership: has anything changed?", **WHFP,** 13.2.76,7
412   Grimond, J (MP) "A 'cynical exercise", **TESS,** 2.5.75, 21
413   Grimond, J (MP) "Devolution could do Scotland more harm than good", **T,** 9.2.76, 12
414   Hamilton, D N H "£35 million a year mystery" (NHS), **SI,** 55 (1975), 3

415 Hargrave, A "How far, how soon?" **Q5** (1976), 6-7
416 Hargrave, A "Living in the past will not do for Scotland", **S,** 26.3.76, 11
417 Hargrave, A "Reappraisal of training practice", **S,** 13.2.76, 10
418 Hargrave, A "Scotland and devolution", **S,** 19-20.10.75
419 Hargrave, A "SDA: an instrument of correction", **S,** 20.8.75, 10
420 Hargrave, A "West pricing itself out of labour market", **S,** 14.2.76, 6
421 Harrison, A "The many who have little", **S,** 6.6.75, 8
422 Harrison, D "Assault on the ivory tower", **TESS,** 16.5.75, 20
423 Harvie, C "The devolution of the intellectuals", **New Statesman,** 28.11.75, 665-6
424 Harvie, C "The road from 1885", **Q7** (1976), 5-7
425 Hebert, H "Labour pains at the birth of Scottish devolution", **G,** 15.1.76, 13
426 Heffer, L (MP) "Devolution and the Labour Party", **New Statesman,** 19.12.75, 777-8
427 Hewitson, J "Sad, scarred face of Portavadie", **GH,** 31.3.76, 7
428 Hewitson, J "The 'army' plotters - and plans to take over Scotland". **GH,** 24.5.75, 4-5
429 Higgins, J "Doon in Troon", **Spectator,** 3.4.76, 9-10
430 Hitchens, C "Chameleon on a tartan rug", **New Statesman,** 6.6.75, 744-5
431 Hitchens, C "Scotland: nation or state?", **New Statesman,** 12.12.75, 744-5
432 Hodson, HV "Introducing a viceroy for Scotland", **S,** 30.4.76, 12
433 Hood, A "Loaded questions", **S,** 30.11.75
434 Hubbert, J "Platform" (secondary education), **Free Student Press,** Oct. 1975, 7
435 Hughes, R (MP) et al. "Politics and education: a four party round-up", **Scottish EducationJournal,** 58. 25 (1975), 726-9
436 Hume, G "Phantom bombers haunt police", **S,** 18.9.75, 13
437 Hunston, H "Professor keeps the kettle boiling", **GH,** 31.3.76, 7
438 Hunston, H "Ringmaster Ross: is this the final curtain?", **GH,** 26.3.76, 7
439 Hunter, A (MP) "Change of strategy and the nationalists go a wooing", **Scottish Miner,** Feb. 1976, 2
440 Hunter, A (MP) "SNP take time to show interest in coal debate", **Scottish Miner,** March 1976, 8
441 Hunter, J "The crofting question", **Q6** (1976), 11-12
442 Hunter, J "The industrial Highlands", **APJ** 506.4.76
443 Hunter, W "A salvo of drama starts a stormy new season on the Islay run", **GH,** 23.2.76, 7
444 Hunter, W "'No', to Europe and on with the ceileidh", **GH,** 5.6.75, 7
445 Hunter, W "Retreat of a reluctant revolutionary", **GH,** 13.2.76, 7
447 Hunter, W "Tall man for a tall job", **GH,** 20.1.76, 7
448 Hunter, W "The professor produces a fine collection of planning foul-ups", **GH,** 30.5.75, 7
449 Hunter, W; Donald, J "Hunter's Aberdeen walk", **GH,** 20-23.10.75
450 Hunter, Gordon, P "High tide for Ocean span?", **GH,** 12.8.75, 6

451 Hunter Gordon, P "Bridge to North must not fall under axe", **GH,** 12.8.75, 6
452 Hutchison, D "Less Scottish parochialism", **Listener,** 19.2.76, 209
453 Imrie, I "Black eye for the militant left", **GH,** 19.11.75, 7
454 Imrie, I "Are union militants a privileged elite?", **GH,** 21.8.75, 6
455 Imrie, I "Cambuslang: a plan for the future", **GH,** 1.7.75, 7
456 Imrie, I "James Jack, still going forward with Labour", **GH,**11.12.75, 7
457 Imrie, I "Jimmy Reid faces defeat in union poll", **GH,** 18.10.75, 5
458 Imrie, I "Scotland is left at the post", **GH,** 3.10.75, 7
459 Jack, I et al. "How Maxwell sabotaged the workers' dream", **ST,** 21.9.75, 17-18
460 Jay, P "Implanting an English heart in the Celtic breast", **T,** 4.12.75, 19
461 Johnston, J "Ferry row leaves a tangle in the isle", **S,** 2.7.75, 11
462 Johnston, J "Rural bus services could be cut again", **Scotsman Half Yearly Review,** (Jan.-June 1975) , 7
463 Johnston, R (MP) "Why Scotland can't afford to come out", **S,** 2.6.75
464 Jones, G "SNP take seat" **S,** 10.7.75, 11
465 Jones, M "What Labour's rebel Scots stand for", **ST,** 11.1.76
466 Jones, RV "Devolution: some pros and cons", **TESS,** 13.6.75, 1-2
467 Kemp, A "The case for confederalism", **S,** 23.2.76, 6
468 Kernohan, RD "Scotland 1976", **Life & Work,** Jan. 1976, 5
469 Kerr, A J C "Second house as part of Assembly?", SI 60 (1976, 3
470 Kerr, J "Devolution comes a long way", **G,** 30.4.76, 6
471 Kerr, J "Press lord", **G,** 17.9.75, 13
472 Kerr, J "Tartan bitter", **G,** 24.9.75, 13
473 Kidston, B "The SNP and the Market", **Scottish Worker,** 2,3 (1975) , 4
474 Kinsey, R & Himsworth, C "Home rule for community councils", **S,** 30.3.76, 10
475 Leigh, A "The new face of Scotland", **Observer,** 1.6.75, 25
476 Leigh, D "Growing pile of devolution theories", **I,** 20.4.76, 2
477 Leigh, D "Continuous high unemployment may diminish usefulness of incentives", **T,** 21.4.76
478 Lindsay, I "Red rimmed eyes on Scotland and the SNP", SI 51 (1975), 5 (review of **The Red Paper on Scotland,** ed. G Brown)
479 Lindsay, S "But this island is coming to life again" (Vatersay), **GH,** 17.7.75, 7
480 Lindsay, S "Oil boom islands join scramble for money", **GH,** 4.9.75, 7
481 Lindsay, S "The regional way of sorting out a transport nightmare", **GH,** 31.1.76, 7
482 Lord Birsay "Why I believe in Scotland ", **Evening News,** 21.11.75, 16
483 Lord Elgin; Lord Mansfield "The noble art of survival", **GH,** 22-23.7.75
484 Lord Ferrier:Letter: devolution referendum **Life & Work,** Feb. 1976,6
485 Lord Wheatley "The law and and Assembly", **S,** 29.1.76, 11
486 McAlpine, T "Defender of the working man", **SI,** 50 (1975) , 1

487 Macauley, D Interview, **WHFP,** 16.1.76, 3
489 MacCalman, J "Crisis? What crisis?", **GH,** 26.1.76, 7
490 MacCormick, N "Two stranded support for legislative devolution", **S,** 5-6.2.76, 7
492 Macdonald, M "The UK need not fear breakup if Scotland gets the right kind of self government", **T,** 18.12.75, 12
493 Macdonald, M "What we want . . . and what we are likely to get", **Evening News,** 26.10 75, 12
494 McElhone, F (MP) Interview, **Scottish Educational Journal,** 59,3 (1976), 12-4
496 MacEwen, L "A new tomorrow for West Highlands' agriculture?", **WHFP,** 25.7.75, 2 and 1.8.75, 2
497 Macfarlane, J "Scottish Liberals can earn the glory if not the power", **S,** 11.3.76, 10
498 McGahey, M "SLP", **Scottish Miner,** Feb. 1976, 4-5
499 McGavin, S "Nothing but heather?", **Contact** (Dundee University), 1,2 (1976), 11-12
500 McGilvray "Sowing the seeds of conflict", **S,** 10.12.75, 12
501 McIlvanney, H "The Scottish Connection", 2.11.75, 11
502 Macintosh, F "Now is the chance to free our education from anglocentrism", **SI,** 53 (1975), 9
503 McIntosh, S "Devolution and the universities". **Morning Star,** 15.12.75, 2
504 McIntyre, A "Education under the Assembly", **Scottish Educational Journal,** 58,24 (1975), 696-7
505 Mackay, G A "Highland Board: a time to flex its muscles", **S,** 31.1.76, 8
506 Mackay, G A "Sharing out the oil bonnza", **G,** 23.6.75, 13
507 Mackenzie, M "Devolution: Australian precedent", **TESS,** 9.5.75, 22
508 McKie, D "Devolutionary dilemmas", **G,** 21.11.75, 10
509 McKillop, J "Collapse of the house empire that John built", (Clyde Valley Estate Agency), **GH,** 6.8.75, 7
510 McKillop, J "Clyde Valley and the £5000 'Partnership' offers", **GH,** 8.8.75, 7
511 McKillop, J "No complaints from Scotland's Ombudsman", **GH,** 30.8.75, 5
512 McKillop, J "Poor health and danger are fruits of oil boom", **GH,** 5.9.75, 7
513 McKillop, J "Provost under pressure" (Farquhar, Dundee), **GH,** 15.3.76, 7
514 McKillop, J "The clearances, 1975", **GH,** 22.8.75, 7
515 McKinlay, J "Campbeltown: the town that missed out on the oil boom", **GH,** 24.3.76, 7
516 McKinlay, J "Hard facts that ended a dream", **GH,** 7.11.75, 6
517 MacKinnon, K "A gaelic revival", **New Society,** 11.3.76, 562-3
518 Mackintosh, J P (MP) "A sound basic structure on which to build", **S,** 28.11.75, 14
519 Mackintosh, J P (MP) "Constituency politics in decay: lessons of Newham", **S,** 21.7.76, 6 (letter 26.6.75)

520 Mackintosh, J P (MP) "Democracy: that's the case for our own parliament", **Evenings News,** 24.11.75, 8
522 Mackintosh, J P (MP) "Devolution fall out", **S,** 19.1.76, 8
523 Mackintosh, J P (MP) "Electoral reform: will PR solve our problems?", **S,** 15.9.75, 6
524 Mackintosh, J P (MP) "Federalism without faults", **S,** 29.3.76, 8
525 Mackintosh, JP (MP) "Labour and Scotland", **New Statesman,** 16.1.76, 55-6
526 Mackintosh, J P (MP) "Making the maximum mess of devolution", **S,** 24.11.75, 6.
527 Mackintosh, J P (MP) "Obstacles to an effective Assembly", **S,** 8.12.75
528 Mackintosh, J P (MP) "Scotland for aye", **New Statesman,** 5.3.76, 281 (letter, 19.3.76, 358-9)
529 Mackintosh, J P (MP) "Strength through collaboration", 21.6.75, 13
530 Mackintosh, J P (MP) "What's to be done about local government?", **S,** 1.9.75, 6
531 MacLean, C "Inspectorate 1976", **TESS,** 30.1-13.2.76
532 Macleod, C "Labour's civil war over crofting lands", **S,** 22.7.75, 8
533 McLeod, M "Women's emergence in the life and politics of a new Scotland", **SI,** 55 (1975), 9
534 McPherson, A "Settling accounts", **TESS,** 30.5.75, 17
535 MacPherson, S "Scottish self-sufficiency", **Spectator,** 14.2.76, 9
536 MacPherson, S "Wake up, Mr Wilson", **Spectator,** 6.12.75, 721-2
537 McRae, T "Oil, an alternative view", **Q6** (1976), 15-17
538 Macrae, W "The thoughts of Mr Macrae", **WHFP,** 30.5.75, 2 (EEC)
539 Mackie, L "Sergeant Lovett, Kishorn's lone ranger", **G,** 28.5.75, 12
540 Mackie, L "Where Skye proves the limits", **G,** 12.5.75, 13
541 Marks, L "Shetlanders match up to the oil moguls", **Observer,** 28.12.75
542 Maxwell, S "Scotland's future lies in the oil", **Daily Telegraph,** 11.12.75, 16
543 Meek, B "Time to shed a tier", **S,** 16.8.75, 8
544 Miller, W "The Scottish voter", **S,** 14-16.10.75
545 Mitchell, J B D "The significance of June 5th", **WS,** 14.6.75, 2
546 Moonman, E (MP) "Time for plain speaking on Scotland's devolution pipe dream", **T,** 8.9.75, 12
547 Morris, J "The granite bonanza" (Aberdeen), **T,** 3.4.76, 8
548 Morrison, A "For an independent socialist Scotland", **Scottish Worker,** 2,8 (1975), 1, 8
549 Morrison, A "Labour, land and the crofters", **Scottish Worker,** 2,5 (1975), 4-5
550 Munro, N "Go integrated with Labour", **TESS,** 2.4.76, 19
551 Munro, N "SLP Inaugural meeting", **WHFP,** 30.1.76, 7
552 Neil, A Letter: economic devolution, **S,** 8.3.76
553 Parkhouse, G "A proud list of success ... and seeds of failure" (W. Ross), **GH,** 27.3.75, 5
554 Parkhouse, G "Expediency rules: that's the message from Troon",

GH, 29.3.76, 7
555 Parry, M "Wasting of a natural asset", **S,** 27.4.76
556 Perman, R "Janey Buchan goes to war", **WS,** 10.1.76, 6
557 Peschek, D "Senior rides again", **Muncipal Review,** 46,555 (1976), 350
558 Potter, A "Precedent produced vote for separation", **S,** 20.4.76, 9
559 Raffan, K "Devolution debate: preparing for battle", **Spectator,** 15.11.75, 628-9
560 Reid, G 'MP) "A state of flux". **Q5,** (1976), 4-5
561 Reid, G (MP) "We won't be the wreckers", **GH,** 21.1.76, 6
562 Reid, G (MP) "Only a tactical 'no' makes sense", **S,** 2.6.75
563 Reid, H "Academic autonomy", **S,** 5.12.75
564 Reid, H "Assembly of no change", **S,** 23.8.75, 8
565 Reid, H "Communication gap in the classrooms", **S,** 26.1.76
566 Reid, H "Dennis Canavan: frontline combatant", **WS,** 13.3.76, 6
567 Reid, H "Fewer proles on the scholastic rolls" , **S,** 19.8.75
568 Reid, H "Manifesto for unity", **S,** 22.9.75, 6
569 Reid, H "Militant moderate" (James Docherty), **S,** 27.4.76
570 Reid, H "SNP want the scholastic slums named", **S,** 3.6.75, 11
571 Reid, H "Union apologists lost cause", **S,** 10.2.76, 9
572 Reid, H "University gets invigilation committee", **S,** 11.7.75, 13
573 Reid, H "Universities seek hearing on devolution ", **S,** 22.7.75, 9
574 Reid, H "Will Assembly get in the way of Education?", **S,** 28.2.76, 8
575 Rennie, W "Opposing views on regional rates for Strathclyde", **S,** 26.6.75, 11
577 Rifkind, M "An Assembly with real teeth", **Evening News,** 25.11.75, 8
578 Rifkind, M "Genuine role for Assembly", **GH,** 20.1.76, 6
579 Rifkind, M "Nationalism", **Jewish Chronicle,** 23.1.76, 10
580 Rifkind, M "The Tories", **Q2** (1975), 5-7
581 Ritchie, M "Scottish Labour schism", **GH,** 18.12.75, 6
582 Robertson, G "Devolution: illusion and reality", **S,** 3.3.76, 10
583 Robertson, G "Natural devolution", **GH,** 19.1.76, 6
584 Robertson, G "We must have more say in Cabinet", **GH,** 19.1.76, 6
585 Rose, R "Assembly seats: a fair share for all?", **GH,** 12.12.75, 7
586 Rose, R "Devolution on a wing and a prayer", **S,** 14.11.75
587 Rose, R "Scotland and the need for a recurring majority", **S,** 13.3.76, 6
588 Rose, R "Scotland in perspective", **Q4,** (1976), 5-6
589 Rose, R "Scottish Assembly: a dilemma for the nationalists", **T,** 29.5.75, 12
590 Rose, R "State of the parties after local polls", **GH,** 6.2.76, 6
591 Rose, R "Waiting for the nationalist bubble to burst", **T,** 28.5.75, 12
592 Ross, I "A divided Labour Party", **Spectator,** 16.8.75, 209
593 Ross, I "Scottish Tories: problems for Mrs Thatcher", **Spectator,** 20.9.75, 369
594 Ross, I "The end of the story" (SDN), **Spectator,** 15.11.75, 629-30
595 Ross, I "The luck of the nationalists", **Spectator,** 25.10.75, 534-5
596 Roth, A "More details needed in register of MPs interests and business activities", **GH,** 2.12.75, 7

597 Russell, W "Behind the sound of rattling claymores: an empty threat from the SNP", **GH**, 21.11.75, 7

598 Russell, W "Millan steps out from the shadow of Ross", **GH**, 9.4.76, 7

599 Russell, W "State of the Union", **GH**, 6.2.76, 7

600 Saunders, G "Need for safeguard for Scots law in EEC", **Scotsman Half Yearly Review** (Jan. June 1975), 3

601 Saunders, H "The party game in new court", **S**, 25.7.75, 11

602 **Scotsman** "Strathclyde Region", **S**, 19.11.75, supplement

603 **Scotsman** "Tayside Region", **S**, 17.2.76, 11-15

604 Scott, D "Administrative transition without the traumas" (in Dumfries & Galloway), **S**, 29.4.76, 12

605 Scott, D "Authorities seek voice in Brussels", **S**, 30.5.75, 11

606 Scott, D "Chairman who quit blames system", **S**, 12.3.76, 13

607 Scott, D "Concern at top over council jobs", **S**, 29.1.76

608 Scott, D "Convention president fears over-government", **S**, 13.5.75, 9

609 Scott, D "Cost of councils increases tenfold"; **S**, 9.7.75, 11

610 Scott, D "Councils facing tough times", **Scotsman Half Yearly Review** (Jan.-June 1975), 2

611 Scott, D "Councils fear Assembly conflict", **S**, 20.2.76, 13

612 Scott, D "Direct links with EEC wanted", **S**, 26.6.75, 11

613 Scott, D "Distribution of rates support grant 'unfair to rural areas' (in Dumfries & Galloway), **S**, 29.4.76, 14

614 Scott, D "Lothian leads in rack-rating", **S**, 18.12.75, 11

615 Scott, D "No tiers of joy in Grampian", **S**, 17.8.75, 11

616 Scott, D "Regions differ on powers of Assembly", **S**, 30.2.76, 13

617 Scott, D "Role of policy planning", **S**, 5.11.75, 10

618 Scott, D "Roles and relationships of local authorities changing", **S**, 16.5.75, 13

619 Scott, D "SNP read happy omens into by-election victory at Slateford-Hailes", **S**, 11.9.75, 11 (letter: 15.9.75)

620 Scott, D "Scottish (rating) system berated", **S**, 16.10.75, 11

621 Scott, D "Signs of new conflict in the two tier farrago", **S**, 14.1.76, 11

622 Scott, D "The SNP will wither away, says Mr Short", **S**, 25.9.75, 11

623 Scott, D "Tory Supremo hints at new council reform", **S**, 10.9.75, 11

624 Scott, D "Way through the labyrinth", **S**, 20.3.76, 8

625 Scott, D; Kemp, A "How the rates explosion was denoted", **S**, 11.7.75, 12

626 **Scottish Miner** "Why we need a powerful Scottish parliament", **Scottish Miner**, Feb. 1976, 5

627 Scottish National Farmers Union: "Devolution for farming 'largely inappropriate'" **Scottish Farmer**, 10.1.76, 15

628 Scottish National Party: "Answer to a question: No", **SI**, 51 (1975), 1

629 Scottish National Party: "Devolution: a few questions and answers" **SI** 58 (1976), 9

630 Shapiro, D "Third World's rule book" (Scottish dependency), **G**, 26.4.76, 12

631 Shaw, W "Mystery tours by public transport", **S**, 6.1.76, 10
632 Shaw, W "SBG runs into trouble", **S**, 7.1.76, 10
633 Short, E (MP) "Come the devolution" (interview),**ST**,2.11.75.
634 Sillars, J (MP) "Land", **Q3**, (1975), 4
635 Sillars, J (MP) "Salvation lies beyond Europe", **S**, 4.6.75, 13
636 Sillars, J (MP) "Scotland's future inside Europe", **S**, 11.6.75, 13
637 Sillars, J (MP) "Strength in diversity", **GH**, 19.1.76, 6
638 Sime, M "Devolution and the universities", **Free Student Press,**
     Spring 1976, 5-6
639 Smallwood, C "Independence not worth the candle", **S**, 7.11.75
     (Letters: 10,11,14,21.11.75; 3.12.75)
640 Smith, A McC "No panacea for Scots law", **S**, 12.11.75
641 Smith, G "Assembly won't herald the millenium", **S**, 16.6.75, 7
642 Smith, G "Labour prepares to fight for survival in Scotland", **T**, 4.3.76,
     14
643 Smith, G "Reconciling political and economic needs in Scotland"
     (SDA) **T**, 10.12.75, 23
644 Smith, G "Rules that must be laid down before another referendum is
     even considered", **T**, 17.12.75, 12
645 Smith, G "Scotland's mood of confidence not based on oil wealth
     alone", **T**, 9.2.76, 16
646 Smith, G "Taking the friction out of finding money for a Scottish
     Assembly", **T**, 13.1.76
647 Smith, G "The new mood in Scotland over devolution", **T**, 18.12.75, 12
648 Smith, G 'Who does what' disputes that could make a mockery of
     devolution", **T**, 31.10.75
649 Sproat, I (MP) "Assembly bandwagon out of control", **S**, 19.7.75, 6
650 Sproat, I (MP) "Endless dogfight", **GH**, 20.1.76, 6
651 Sproat, I (MP) "The need to stand together", **S**, 3.6.75, 11
652 Sproat, I (MP) "Whither the Conservatives?" **S**, 20.10.75, 6
653 Steel, D (MP) "Splitting up the power - sensibly", **Evening News,**
     26.11.75, 12
654 Steel, D (MP) "Wanted: scope to develop Scotland in the way we
     want", **GH**, 21.11.75, 6
655 Steel, D (MP) "Why Scotland will brook no more delay on
     devolution", **T**, 26.11.75, 16
656 Stewart, D (MP) "A true nationalist faith", **SI** 52 (1975), 5
657 Stewart, D (MP) "Westminster revealed as the enemy of Scotland",
     SI 54 (1975), 9
658 Stoddart, C "Crime and the courts", **Q4,** (1976), 12-14
659 Tait, R:Interview (on SLP) **Aberdeen People's Press,** 55 (1976), 8-9
660 Taylor, T (MP) "These are the problems we would face", **Evening
     News,** 25.11.75, 8
661 Thompson, A "Case for cooperation", **S**, 9.12.75
662 Thompson, A "Civil servants await new role", **GH**, 9.10.75, 7
663 Thompson, F "Land", **Calcagus** 3 (1976), 10
664 Thomson, C "A vicious circle of deprivation that is threatening

education", **GH,** 16.9.75, 7

665 Thomson, C "Bruce Millan and the Stonehouse dilemma", **GH,** 16.4.76, 7

666 Thomson, C "Fateful weekend as Strathclyde decides on spending cuts", **GH,** 13.1.76, 7

667 Thomson, C "Forward without the people", **GH,** 7.8.75, 7

668 Thomson, C "How can council spending be brought under control?", **GH,** 31.10.75, 7

669 Thomson, C "How Strathclyde cut back to hold down rates", **GH,** 4.3.76, 7

670 Thomson, C "'Scapegoat' Strathclyde", **GH,** 19.8.75, 6

671 Thomson, C "Tories hold the key at East Kilbride", **GH,** 2.2.76, 7

672 Thomson, C "When man cannot live by money alone", **GH,** 4.7.75, 7

673 Thorburn, I et al. "The devolution debate", **TESS,**20.6.75, 1-3, 14.15

674 Thornton, F O "Trafficking in our future," **S,** 20.4.76

675 Trevor-Roper, H "Scotching the myths of devolution", **T,** 28.4.76

676 Trotter, S "No ripple as Millan takes over in devolution special", **GH,** 15.4.76, 7

677 Trotter, S "Not dying - just about to fade away - the office of Secretary of State", **GH,** 24.10.75, 7

678 Tur, R H S "Devolution and the House of Lords", **Scots Law Times,** 7.5.76, 133-4

679 Tur, R H S "Harnessing local energies through community councils", **GH,** 23.9.75, 6

680 Vassie, J D "Europe and the Scottish dimension", **S,** 22.5.75, 10

681 Walker, W G "Can a class-free party carry a 'social-democratic' tag?", **SI** 60 (1976), 5

682 Wapshott, N "Soul searching for the Scots socialists", **S,** 17.2.76, 9

683 Wapshott, N "Young Scots face 'permanent unemployment'", **S,** 24-25.9.75

684 Warden, J "Assembly by fits and starts", **GH,** 16.6.75, 6

685 Warden, J "Scotland: Labour's rogue electorate", **GH,** 21.7.75, 6

686 Warden, J "The price tag on devolution", **GH,** 26.5.75, 6

687 Waterhouse, R "Beauty belies the Borders", **G,** 30.4.76, 7

688 Watkins, A "The great devolution muddle", **New Statesman,** 19.10.75, 458

689 Watkins, A "Willie Ross for King", **New Statesman,** 28.11.75, 662

690 West, A "Women in Scottish society", **Masque** (Glasgow), April 1976, 40-41

691 Woodcock, C "Learning to combat ills of recession", **G,** 30.4.76, 8

692 Waugh, B "Platform" (SNP aid policy), **Free Student Press,** Spring 1976, 8

693 Weir, A D "England expects: Scotland forgets", **TESS,** 6.6.75, 1-2

694 Whale, J "Secret papers cast doubt on Scottish and Welsh Assemblies", **ST,** 28.9.75, 4

695 Whale, J "The arguments Short kept quiet", **ST,** 30.11.75

696 Wilson, B "A barren tract" (crofting), **G,** 7.4.76, 9

697 Wilson, B "An exchange of correspondence" (on Land), **WHFP,** 9.5.76, 7
698 Wilson, B "Fiasco for the workers' paper", **New Statesman,** 24.10.75, 496
699 Wilson, B "Whisky sour", **G,** 29.11.75
700 Wolfe, W "German-Swedish models for us", **SI,** 56 (1975), 6
701 Wolfe, W "Scotland international", **SI** 50 (1975), 5
702 Wolfe, W "Two general elections away is too far away", **SI** 52 (1975), 6
703 Wright, A "Broadcasting home rule", **S,** 2.7.75, 11
704 Wyn Ellis, N "A voice from the ranks" (Tam Dalyell), **Sunday Times Magazine,** 12.10.75, 75-84
705 Yeats, It "Are there too many teachers' organisations?", **GH,** 3.10.75, 7
706 Young, E "The cheap loans affair: an indefensible secrecy", **GH,** 18.9.75, 12
707 Young, G "The case for Stonehouse", **S,** 2.2.76, 8

ADDENDA

103 Scottish National Party: **Industrial policy proposals.** Edinburgh: SNP Industrial Policy Committee, 1976, 6pp
129 Young, E "Planning considerations". **Scots Law Times,** 1975, 245-53
250 Ascherson, N "SNP's lot not a happy one" (at Westminster). **S,** 8.8.75, 11
251 Ascherson, N "State of the Unionists", **S,** 11.7.75, 13
305 Campbell, J S "Public inquiry procedures: new proposals", **Scots Law Times,** 1975, 105-7
307 Chisholm, W "Borders want more people", **Scotsman Half Yearly Review** (Jan-June 1975), 9
343 **Donaldson, A "Tom Gibson"** (SNP founder), **SI** 51 (1975), 6
446 Hunter, W "Scots Tory melting pot casts up man of steel". **GH,** 13.5.75, 6
488 MacCalman, J "Council houses: will Labour dodge a sell-out". **GH,** 16.4.76, 7
491 Macdonald, G "Grampian campaign pays off for the ratepayer". **GH,** 12.2.76, 7
495 MacEwen, J "The struggle to find out — who owns Scotland?". **WHFP,** 25.7.75, 2 and 1.8.75, 2
521 Mackintosh, J P (MP) "Devolution and the UK's death wish". **S,** 27.10.75

Part III: INDEX

Note: Material on devolution and particular aspects of Scottish public affairs will be found under "Devolution". Items with subheadings are in bold type.

MPs 67, 270-71, 330, 360, 435, 492-3, 560-62, 656-7
Secretary of State:
Ross 286, 288, 438, 553, 677
Millan 598, 676
Under-Secretaries 247, 322-3, 494
"Separatism" See Nationalism
Shetland 75, 345, 369, 377-8, 480, 541 (see also Local Government)
Socialism 18, 41, 59, 121, 403, 424, 548 (see also Reid, J.; Nationalism and socialism)
Teachers' organisations 108, 569, 705
"Terrorism" 272, 428, 436, 472
Trades Union movement 18, 53, 101a, 267, 453-4, 456-8
Transport, roads 12, 119, 126, 127, 443, 451, 461, 462, 481, 631-2, 674
Urban problems:
Aberdeen 17, 290, 449, 547 (see also Oil)
Glasgow 80a, 350-51, 437, 672
New Towns 665, 707
Women 28, 118, 271, 533, 690

appendices

1. **THE SCOTTISH OFFICE**

2. **SCOTTISH OFFICE MINISTERS**

3. **SCOTTISH LAW OFFICERS**

4. **POLITICAL PARTIES**

5. **SCOTTISH MEMBERS OF PARLIAMENT**

6. **OCTOBER 1974 GENERAL ELECTION RESULTS**

7. **LOCAL GOVERNMENT DIRECTORY**
   - (a) **Convention of Scottish Local Authorities**
   - (b) **Convention Policy Committee**
   - (c) **May 1974 Local Election Results**
   - (d) **Conveners, Chairmen, Provosts, Chief Executives and addresses of Local Authorities**

Acknowledgements: We would like to thank the following for their help: Scotsman Newspapers; Scottish Office; Scottish Information Office; Convention of Scottish Local Authorities; Scottish Conservative Party; Labour Party; Scottish Liberal Party; Scottish National Party; Planning Department, Edinburgh District Council.

We have made use of information from the following:

The Scottish Local Government Elections 1974, Results and Statistics. J. M. Bochel and D. T. Denver. Scottish Academic Press, 1975.

Her Majesty's Ministers and Senior Staff in Public Departments, No. 8. H.M.S.O., 1976.

Scotland. H.M.S.O., June 1974.

1. THE SCOTTISH OFFICE

New St Andrew's House
St James Centre
Edinburgh
Telephone 031-556 8400

Dover House, Whitehall
London SW1A 2AU
Telephone 01-930 6151

The Secretary of State is directly responsible to Parliament for all the departments making up the Scottish Office. The Scottish Office consists of five departments and number of "central service" units concerned with such matters as finance, legal services, information and personnel services. The five departments are of equal status and each is in the charge of a Secretary who is responsible to the Secretary of State for the work of his department. A Deputy Secretary (Central Services), who ranks equally with the Secretaries of the five departments, has special responsibilities for the co-ordination of work on devolution and the control of central finance functions, including responsibility for local authority finance.

The Permanent Under Secretary of State is the general adviser to the Secretary of State. Under his chairmanship the Heads of Departments and the Deputy Secretary (Central Services) constitute a Management Group to ensure the co-ordination of the work of the Secretary of State's Departments and to consider common problems across the whole field of Scottish Office responsibilities.

Permanent Under Secretary of State
Sir Nicholas Morrison, K.C.B.
Private secretary: D. J. Crawley

Deputy Secretary (Central Services)
W. K. Fraser
Private secretary: Miss A. Anderson

Department of Agriculture and Fisheries for Scotland
St Andrew's House
Edinburgh EH1 3DA
Telephone 031-556 8501

Secretary: J. Smith, C.B.E.

This department is responsible for the promotion of agriculture and the fishing industry. This includes, on the agricultural side, the provision of technical and financial help to farmers, the supervision of educational, advisory and research services, the administration of various schemes for the improvement of land, farm stock and crops, the development of crofting and the management of a large area of State-owned agricultural property. As regards fisheries, duties extend from international relations (including negotiation within the European Community and co-operation in international organisations concerned with the conservation of fish stocks) to domestic matters, such as financial support for the fishing industry, assistance for fishery harbours, scientific research into fisheries' problems and the protection of Scottish fisheries by the department's fleet of fishery cruisers.

Scottish Education Department
New St Andrew's House
St James Centre
Edinburgh EH1 3SY
Telephone 031-556 8400

Secretary: J. M. Fearn

This department, operating through local education authorities and other bodies, supervises the provision of primary, secondary and further education, including school accommodation, the supply of teachers and the development of curricula. It exercises certain responsibilities for Scottish universities, although these, like other universities in Britain, are primarily the concern of the Department of Education and Science; and its functions also cover youth and community services, adult education, sport, physical recreation and the arts. It works closely with the National Museums and Galleries and the National Library of Scotland. The Social Work Services Group, which forms part of the Scottish Education Department, gives advice to local authority social work departments in their statutory duty of providing a range of social and welfare services, provides liaison with voluntary social work organisations and implements the programme of grant aid to local authorities for the provision of special facilities in deprived urban areas.

Scottish Home and Health Department
New St Andrew's House
St James Centre
Edinburgh EH1 3TF
Telephone 031-556 8400

Secretary: R. P. Fraser, C.B.

This department has two main responsibilities. On the home side it is involved in the administration of the police, fire and prison services; it is concerned with criminal justice, the Licensing Acts and legislation relating to public entertainment; and it is responsible for the law relating to the conduct of parliamentary and local elections and the registration of electors, and for a wide range of ceremonial and formal business. On the health side it is responsible for the administration of the National Health Service in Scotland and has a general concern with all matters affecting public health in Scotland. The department also exercises, on behalf of the Secretary of State, functions deriving from the latter's joint responsibility with the Lord Advocate for law reform and for legal aid.

Scottish Development Department
New St Andrew's House
St James Centre
Edinburgh EH1 3SZ
Telephone 031-556 8400

Secretary: K. Lewis, C.B., C.V.O.

This is the central department responsible for general policy relating to local government administration and for town and country planning, housing, roads, water and other environmental services. It is concerned, among other things, with urban development and conservation, with all aspects of housing by local authorities, with the making and amendment of building standard regulations and with the oversight of arrangements for public water supplies, sewerage and sewage disposal, the prevention of air and river pollution and coast and flood protection.

Scottish Economic Planning Department
New St Andrew's House
St James Centre
Edinburgh EH1 3TA
Telephone 031-556 8400

Secretary: T. R. H. Godden, C.B.

This department has taken over what was formerly the Regional Development Division of the Scottish Office, dealing with the formulation of plans for economic development in Scotland and co-ordinating their implementation. It also includes some other closely allied divisions formerly in the Development Department, such as those responsible for relations with the Highlands and Islands Development Board, the Scottish Tourist Board, the Scottish Electricity Board, the Scottish Transport Group (which controls all publicly owned road passenger and shipping operations in Scotland) and the New Town Development Corporations. It is designed to provide the necessary support within the Scottish Office for the Minister of State, who in May 1973 was given co-ordinating responsibilities in relation to oil development in Scotland; and it will also be concerned with the Scottish aspects of regional policies, including those relating to the European Community.

2. SCOTTISH OFFICE MINISTERS

Secretary of State
Bruce Millan, M.P.
Private Secretary: N. J. Shanks

Minister of State (Commons)
Responsible for Economic Planning and Oil Development:
Gregor McKenzie, M.P.
Private Secretary: J. S. Graham

Minister of State (Lords)
Responsible for Development and E.E.C. matters: Lord Kirkhill
Private Secretary: L. C. Cunning

Parliamentary Under Secretary
Responsible for Agriculture, Fisheries and Housing: Hugh Brown, M.P.
Private Secretary: C C. Forsyth

Parliamentary Under Secretary
Responsible for Health, Education and Social Work Services: Frank McElhone, M.P.
Private Secretary: Mrs M. J. Martyn

Parliamentary Under Secretary
Responsible for Devolution and Home Affairs: Harry Ewing, M.P.
Private Secretary: D. I. Dalgetty

3. SCOTTISH LAW OFFICERS

Lord Advocate
Chief legal adviser on Scottish questions and principal representative of Crown for purposes of litigation: Ronald King Murray, M.P.

Solicitor General for Scotland
Second law officer of the Crown: John McCluskey, Q.C.

4. POLITICAL PARTIES

SCOTTISH LABOUR PARTY
Room 267
12 Waterloo Street
Glasgow
Telephone: 041-248 7104
General Secretary: Alex Neil

THE LABOUR PARTY
Scottish Council
Keir Hardie House
1 Lyndoch Place
Glasgow G3 6AB
Telephone: 041 332 8946-7
Scottish Organiser and Secretary: Jim McGrandle
Assistant Scottish Organiser and Womens Organiser: Mrs Ann Urquhart
Assistant Scottish Organiser and Youth Officer: James Allison
Chairman: Mrs Charlotte Haddow
Research Assistant: Douglas Herbison
Press Officer: Mr Douglas Machray

SCOTTISH LIBERAL PARTY
2 Atholl Place
Edinburgh EH3 8HS
Telephone: 031 229 7484-5
President: Lady Bannermann
Leader: Russell Johnston MP
Chairman: W. Menzies Campbell
Deputy Chairman: David Miller, Forbes McCallum, Mrs Kathleen Smith
Joint Treasurers: John Lambie, Lt. Col. Patrick Lord- Philips

COMMUNIST PARTY
Gallacher House
69 Albert Road
Glasgow GH2 8DP
Telephone: 041-423 1276
Scottish Organiser: Mr O'Donnell

SCOTTISH CONSERVATIVE PARTY
11 Atholl Crescent
Edinburgh EH3 8HG
Telephone: 031 229 1342
Director of Scottish Conservative Party: Mr A. M. Graham Macmillan
President Scottish Conservative and Unionist Association: Mr Ronald Anderson, MA, LLb
Senior Vice President: Mr T. N. H. Young MBE
Junior Vice President: Mr C. Russell Sanderson
Honorary Treasurer: Mr Ronald S. McNeill
Honorary Secretary: Mr H. C. Beveridge OBE,
Mr James B. Highgate, MA, LLB
Secretary: Mr Andrew Strang MBE

SCOTTISH NATIONAL PARTY
6 North Charlotte Street
Edinburgh EH2 4JH
Telephone: 031 226 3661
President: Dr Robert McIntyre
Chairman: William Wolfe
National Secretary: Miss Muriel Gibson
Press Officer: Stephen Maxwell
Research Officer: Donald Bain
National Organiser: John McAteer
Industrial Officer: Stephen Butler

5. SCOTTISH MEMBERS OF PARLIAMENT

The 71 MP.s who represent Scottish Constituencies are listed below in alphabetical order:

Bain, Mrs Margaret (Dunbartonshire, East) S.N.P.

Bray, Dr Jeremy (Motherwell and Wishaw) Lab.

Brown, Mr Hugh (Glasgow, Queen's Park) Lab.

Buchan, Mr Norman (Renfrewshire, West) Lab.

Buchanan-Smith, Mr Alick (Angus, North and Mearns) Cons.

Campbell, Mr Ian (Dunbartonshire, West) Lab.

Canavan, Mr Dennis (West Stirlingshire) Lab.

Carmichael, Mr Neil (Glasgow, Kelvingrove) Lab.

Cook, Mr Robin (Edinburgh Central) Lab.

Corrie, Mr John (Bute and North Ayrshire) Cons.

Craigen, Mr J. M. (Glasgow, Maryhill) Lab.-Coop.

Crawford, Mr Douglas (Perth and East Perthshire) S.N.P.

Dalyell, Mr Tam (West Lothian) Lab.

Dempsey, Mr James (Coatbridge and Airdrie) Lab.

Doig, Mr Peter (Dundee, West) Lab.

Douglas-Hamilton, Lord James (Edinburgh, West) Cons.

Eadie, Mr Alex (Midlothian) Lab.

Ewing, Mr Harry (Stirling, Falkirk and Grangemouth) Lab.

Ewing, Mrs Winifred (Moray and Nairn) S.N.P.

Fairbairn, Mr Nicholas (Kinross and West Perthshire) Cons.

Fairgrieve, Mr Russell (Aberdeenshire, West) Cons.

Fletcher, Mr Alexander (Edinburgh, North) Cons.

Galbraith, Mr T. G. D. (Glasgow, Hillhead) Cons.

Galpern, Sir M. (Glasgow, Shettleston) Lab.

Gilmour, Sir John (Fife, East) Cons.

Gourlay, Mr Harry (Kirkcaldy) Lab.

Gray, Mr Hamish (Ross and Cromarty) Cons.

Grimond, Mr Jo (Orkney and Shetland) Lib.

Hamilton, Mr James (Bothwell) Lab.

Hamilton, Mr William (Fife, Central) Lab.

Hart, Mrs Judith (Lanark) Lab.

Harvie Anderson, Mrs B. (Renfrewshire, East) Cons.

Henderson, Mr Douglas (Aberdeenshire, East) S.N.P.

Hughes, Mr Robert (Aberdeen, North) Lab.

Hunter, Mr Adam (Dunfermline) Lab.

Hutchison, Mr Michael Clark (Edinburgh, South) Cons.

Johnston, Mr Russell (Inverness) Lib.

Lambie, Mr David (Central Ayrshire) Lab.

Mabon, Dr J. Dickson (Greenock and Port Glasgow) Lab-Coop.

McCartney, Mr Hugh (Dunbartonshire, Central) Lab.

MacCormick, Mr Ian (Argyll) S.N.P.

McElhone, Mr Frank (Glasgow, Queen's Park) Lab.

MacKenzie, Mr Gregor (Rutherglen) Lab.

Mackintosh, Mr John P. (Berwick and East Lothian) Lab.

Maclennan, Mr Robert (Caithness and Sutherland) Lab.

McMillan, Mr Tom (Glasgow, Central) Lab.

Millan, Mr Bruce (Glasgow, Craigton) Lab.

Miller, Dr M. S. (East Kilbride) Lab.

Monro, Mr Hector (Dumfries) Cons.

Reid, Mr George (Clackmannan and East Stirlingshire) S.N.P.

Rifkind, Mr Malcolm (Edinburgh, Pentlands) Cons.

Robertson, Mr John (Paisley) S.L.P.

Ross, Mr William (Kilmarnock) Lab.

Selby, Mr Harry (Glasgow, Govan) Lab.

Sillars, Mr James (South Ayrshire) S.L.P.

Small, Mr William (Glasgow, Garscadden) Lab.

Smith, Mr John (Lanarkshire, North) Lab.

Sproat, Mr Iain (Aberdeen, South) Cons.

Steel, Mr David (Roxburgh, Selkirk and Peebles) Lib.

Stewart, Mr Donald (Western Isles) S.N.P.

Strang, Dr Gavin (Edinburgh, East) Lab.

Taylor, Mr Teddy (Glasgow, Cathcart) Cons.

Thompson, Mr George (Galloway) S.N.P.

Watt, Mr Hamish (Banff) S.N.P.

Welsh, Mr Andrew (South Angus) S.N.P.

White, Mr James (Glasgow, Pollok) Lab.

Wilson, Mr Alexander (Hamilton) Lab.

Wilson, Mr Gordon (Dundee, East) S.N.P.

Younger, Mr George (Ayr) Cons.

6. OCTOBER 1974 GENERAL ELECTION RESULTS

OCTOBER 1974 GENERAL ELECTION RESULTS FOR SCOTLAND (71 SEATS)

	Total Votes	Per Cent Share	State of Parties
Labour	1,000,551	36.28%	41 seats
SNP	839,617	30.44%	11 seats
Conservative	681,331	24.71%	16 seats
Liberal	228,855	8.30%	3 seats
Communist	7,453	0.27%	0 seats

We list here the results in Scottish constituencies giving the name and party of the winner and his majority. Results are given for the four cities and then alphabetically for the remaining seats.

ABERDEEN	Majority
Aberdeen, North	
R Hughes (Lab)	9,621
Aberdeen, South	
I Sproat (Cons)	365
DUNDEE	
Dundee, East	
G Wilson (SNP)	6,983
Dundee, West	
P Doig (Lab)	2,802
EDINBURGH	
Edinburgh, Central	
R Cook (Lab)	3,953
Edinburgh, East	
Dr G S Strang (Lab)	8,456
Edinburgh, Leith	
R K Murray (Lab)	3,445
Edinburgh, North	
A Fletcher (Cons)	4,391
Pentlands	
M Rifkind (Cons)	1,237
Edinburgh, South	
A M Clark-Hutchison (Cons)	3,226
Edinburgh, West	
Lord J Douglas-Hamilton (Cons)	5,202

A	
Aberdeenshire, East	
D Henderson (SNP)	4,371
Aberdeenshire, West	
T R Fairgrieve (Cons)	2,468
Angus, North and Mearns	
A L Buchanan-Smith (Cons)	2,551
Angus, South	
A Welsh (SNP)	1,824

GLASGOW	
Cathcart	
E Taylor (Cons)	1,757
Glasgow, Central	
T McMillan (Lab)	6,441
Glasgow, Craigton	
B Millan (Lab)	8,781
Glasgow, Garscadden .	
W W Small (Lab)	7,637
Glasgow, Govan	
H Selby (Lab)	1,952
Glasgow, Hillhead	
T G D Galbraith (Cons)	2,696
Glasgow, Kelvingrove	
N G Carmichael (Lab)	4,119
Glasgow, Maryhill	
J Craigen (Lab)	9,418
Glasgow, Pollock	
J White (Lab)	7,091
Glasgow, Provan	
H D Brown (Lab)	9,974
Glasgow, Queens Park	
F McElhone (Lab)	8,914
Glasgow, Shettleston	
Sir M Galpern (Lab)	6,349
Glasgow, Springburn	
R Buchanan (Lab)	8,395

Argyll	
I S M MacCormick (SNP)	3,931
Ayr	
G Younger (Cons	3,219
Ayrshire Central	
D Lambie (Lab)	9,555
Ayrshire South	
J Sillars (Lab)	14,478

142

B
Banffshire
H Watt (SNP) — 1,851
Berwick and East Lothian
J P Mackintosh (Lab) — 2,740
Bothwell
J Hamilton (Lab) — 10,948
Bute and Ayrshire
J A Corrie (Cons) — 3,506

C
Caithness and Sutherland
R A MacLennan (Lab) — 2,560
Clackmannan and East Stirling
G N Reid (SNP) — 7,341
Coatbridge and Airdrie
J Dempsey (Lab) — 10,568

D
Dumfries
H Munro (Cons) — 5,828
Dunbartonshire, Central
H McCartney (Lab) — 4,385
Dunbartonshire, East
Mrs M Bain (SNP) — 22
Dunbartonshire, West
L Campbell (Lab) — 1,184
Dunfermline
A Hunter (Lab) — 5,291

E
East Kilbride
Dr M Millar (Lab) — 2,704

F
Fife Central
W W Hamilton (Lab) — 7,986
Fife, East
Sir J Gilmour (Cons) — 3,914

G
Galloway
G H Thompson (SNP) — 30
Greenock and Port Glasgow
Dr J D Mabon (Lab) — 11,933

H
Hamilton
A Wilson (Lab) — 3,332

I
Inverness-shire
R Johnstone (Lib) — 1,134

K
Kilmarnock
W Ross (Lab) — 7,529

Kinross and West Perthshire
N H Fairbairn (Cons) — 53
Kirkcaldy
H P Gourlay (Lab) — 6,101

L
Lanark
Mrs Judith Hart, (Lab) — 698
Lanarkshire, North
J Smith (Lab) — 8,341

M
Midlothian
A Eadie (Lab) — 4,084
Moray & Nairn
Mrs W M Ewing (SNP) — 367
Motherwell and Wishaw
Dr J Bray (Lab) — 4,962

O
Orkney and Shetland
J Grimmond (Lib) — 6,832

P
Paisley
J Robertson (Lab) — 5,590
Perth and East Perthshire
D Crawford (SNP) — 793

R
Renfrewshire East
Mrs B H Anderson (Cons) — 8,710
Renfrewshire West
N Buchan (Lab) — 5,300
Ross and Cromarty
H Gray (Cons) — 663
Roxburgh, Selkirk and Peebles
D M S Steel (Lib) — 7,433
Rutherglen
J G MacKenzie (Lab) — 7,356

S
Stirling, Falkirk and Grangemouth
H Ewing (Lab) — 1,766
Stirlingshire, West
D A Canavan (Lab) — 367

W
Western Isles
D J Stewart (SNP) — 5,232
West Lothian
T Dalyell (Lab) — 2,690

143

7. LOCAL GOVERNMENT DIRECTORY

(a) Convention of Scottish Local Authorities

(a) CONVENTION OF SCOTTISH LOCAL AUTHORITIES
3 Forres Street
Edinburgh EH3 6BL
Telephone: 031-225 1626/7
Secretary/Treasurer: Graham H. Spiers, M.A., LL.B.

(b) Convention Policy Committee

CONVENTION POLICY COMMITTEE (28 members)
Chairman: Councillor G. Sharp
Vice-chairman: vacant

REGIONS:

Borders: Councillor J. M. Askew, C.B.E.
Central: Councillor J. Anderson
Dumfries and Galloway: Councillor J. F. Niven, C.B.E.
Fife: Councillor G. Sharp, O.B.E.
Grampian: Councillor A. F. Mutch
Highland: Councillor M. J. Nicolson
Lothian: Councillors P. Wilson and G. Foulkes
Strathclyde: Councillors C. Gray, C. O'Halloran, G. M. Shaw, R. Stewart.
Tayside: Councillor A. M. Manson
Western Isles: Councillor D. Macaul.ay

DISTRICT:
Angus: Councillor L. Gray-Cheape
Caithness: Councillor J. M. Young
Cumnock and Doon Valley: Councillor T. P. McIntyre
Edinburgh: Councillor R. M. Knox
Falkirk: Provost W. Ure
Glasgow: Councillors D. Dynes and D. Hodge
Gordon: Councillor J. B. Presley
Kirkcaldy: Councillor R. King
Monklands: Councillor T. Clarke
Moray: Councillor J. M. Anderson
Perth and Kinross: Councillor J. D. Young
Renfrew: Provost E. Conway
Stirling: Councillor Mrs L. M. McCraig

(c)   May 1974 Local Election Results

REGIONAL SUMMARY TABLE

SEATS WON

	Cons	Lab	Lib	SNP	Ind	Comm	Others
Highland	2	4	3	1	37	—	–
Grampian	28	13	2	—	10	—	–
Tavside	22	15	—	—	9	—	–
Fife	10	26	—	—	3	1	2
Lothian	19	24	1	3	1	—	1
Central	4	17	—	9	3	—	1
Borders	7	—	3	—	13	—	–
Strathclyde	20	71	2	5	5	—	–
Dumfries and Galloway	—	2	—	—	33	—	–
	112	172	11	18	114	1	4

DISTRICT SUMMARY TABLE

SEATS WON

	Cons	Lab	Lib	SNP	Ind	Comm	Others
Highland★	—	4	2	4	99	—	–
Grampian	25	30	4	1	48	...	—
Tayside	43	29	—	—	21	—	1
Fife	24	43	1	2	10	—	4
Lothian	38	62	3	8	5	—	1
Central	9	29	—	21	8	—	1
Borders	9	1	—	—	44	—	–
Strathclyde	92	225	7	25	49	—	8
Dumfries and Galloway	1	5	—	1	61	—	2
	241	428	17	62	345	—	17

★No candidates in 5 wards

145

(d) Conveners, Chairmen, Provosts, Chief Executives and

addresses of Local Authorities

Region	Convener	Chief Executive	Telephone
BORDERS	J M Askew CBE BA JP	K J Clark BordersRegional Council Regional Headquarters Newton St Boswells Roxburghshire TD6 0SA	083 52 3301
Berwickshire District:	Chairman: James R Ford	D Dunn Berwickshire District Council Council Offices 8 Newton Street Duns Berwickshire TD11 3DU	036 12 2331
Ettrick and Lauderdale District:	Chairman George R Johnstone	D H Cowan Ettrick and Lauderdale District Council Council Chambers Paton Street Galashiels TD1 3AS	0896 4751
Roxburgh District:	Chairman David Atkinson	W C Hogg Roxburgh District Council Offices High Street Hawick Roxburghshire TD9 9EF	0450 2347
Tweedale District:	Chairman Thomas Blyth	G Gardiner Tweedale District Council Rosetta Road Peebles	0721 20153

Region	Convener	Chief Executive	Telephone
CENTRAL	James Anderson	E Geddes Central Regional Council Viewforth Stirling FK8 2ET	0786 3111

146

| Clackmannan District: | **Chairman**
Daniel A. McDonald | A Stewart
Clackmannan District Council
The Whins
Alloa
SK10 3RG | 025 92 2160 |

| Falkirk District: | **Provost**
William Ure | J P H Paton
Falkirk District Council
Muncipal Buildings
Falkirk
FK1 5RS | 0324 24911 |

| Stirling District: | **Chairman**
Mrs Laura McCaig | D M Bowie
Stirling District Council
Muncipal Buildings
Stirling
FK0 0HU | 0786 3131 |

Region	**Convener**	**Chief Executive**	**Telephone**
DUMFRIES & GALLOWAY	John F Niven CBE	L T Carnegie Dumfries & Galloway Regional Council Council Offices English Street Dumfries DG1 2DD	0387 3141

| Annandale and Eskdale
District: | **Chairman**
R G Greenhov | G F Murray
Annandale and Eskdale
District Council
Council Chambers
Annan
Dumfries-shire
DG12 6QA | 04612 3311 |

| Nithsdale District: | **Chairman**
Frank Young | G D Grant
Nithsdale District Council
Muncipal Chambers
Dumfries
DG1 2AD | 0387 3166 |

| Stewarty District: | Convener
Ronald Maxwell | W L Dick-Smith
Stewarty District Council
Council Offices
Kirkcudbright
DG6 4PJ | Kirkudbright
30291 |

| Wigtown District: | **Chairman**
David R Robertson | D R Wilson
Wigtown District Council
Sun Street
Stranraer
DG9 7JJ | 0776 2151 |

147

Region	Convener	Chief Executive	Telephone
FIFE	George Sharp	J M Dunlop Fife Regional Council Fife House North Street Glenrothes Fife KY7 5LT	
Dunfermline District·	**Provost** Leslie Wood	G Brown Dunfermline District Council City Chambers Dunfermline Fife 7ND	0383 22711
Kirkcaldy District:	**Convener** Robert King	C D Chapman OBE Kirkcaldy District Council Town House Kirkcaldy KY1 1XW	0592 61144
North East Fife District:	**Chairman** Cpt Douglas M Rusell	H Farquhar North East Fife District Council County Buildings Cupar Fife KY15 4 TA	0334 3772

Region	Convener	Chief Executive	Telephone
GRAMPIAN	Alexander F Mutch	J L Russell Grampian Regional Council County Buildings 22 Union Terrace Aberdeen AB9 1HJ	0224 23444
Banff and Buchan District:	**Chairman** W R Cruickshank	N. S. McAllister Banff and Buchan District Council St Leonards Sandyhill Road Banff AB4 1BH	026 12 2521
City of Aberdeen District:	**Lord Provost** Robert S Lennox	J F Watt City of Aberdeen District Council Town House Aberdeen AB9 1 AQ	0224 23456

Gordon District:	**Chairman** James B Presly	A C Kennedy Gordon District Council 3 High Street Inverurie Aberdeenshire AB5 9QA	04672 3423
Kincardine and Deeside District:	**Chairman** Ian W Frain	Mrs E M G Cockburn Kincardine and Deeside District Council Viewmount Ardithie Road Stonehaven AB3 2DQ	056 92 2001
Moray District:	**Chairman** James M Anderson	J P O Boll Moray District Council District Headquarters High Street Elgin Morayshire IV30 1BX	0343 3451

Region	Convener	Chief Executive	Telephone
HIGHLAND	Rev Murdo J Nicolson	F G Armstrong Highland Regional Council Regional Buildings Glen Urquhart Road Inverness IV3 5NX	0463 34121
Badenoch and Strathespy District:	**Chairman** Major AC Robertson MBE	Henry G McCulloch Badenoch and Strathspey District Council Council Offices High Street Kingussie Inverness-shire	Kingussie 441
Caithness District:	**Chairman** John M Young	A Beattie Caithness District Council District Offices Wick Caithness KW1 4AB	0955 2233
Inverness District:	**Provost** I C Fraser	I J Miller Inverness District Council Townhouse Inverness IV1 1JJ	0463 39111

Lochaber District:	**Chairman** Colonel James W Forbes MBE	J T Ballantyne Lochaber District Council Tweeddale Fort William Inverness-shire PH33 6EL	
Nairn District:	**Provost** Lt Col Hugh McLean MBE	J Ramund McCluskey Nairn District Council Court House Lane Nairn IV12 4DR	066 75 205€
Ross and Cromarty District:	**Chairman** Earl of Cromartie MC	T M Aitchison Ross and Cromarty District Council County Buildings Dingwall IV15 9QH	0349 338】
Skye and Lochalsh District:	**Chairman** Roderick S Budge	David Noble Skye and Lochalsh District Council Dunvegan Road Portree Isle of Skye IV51 9HJ	Portree 44】
Sutherland District:	**Chairman** Colonel A M Gilmour	D W Martin Sutherland District Council District Offices Golspie Suterland KW10 6RB	Golspie 39:
Region LOTHIAN	**Convener** Peter Wilson	**Chief Executive** R G E Peggie Lothian Regional Council Council Headquarters George IV Bridge Edinburgh	**Telephone** 031 229 929:
City of Edinburgh District:	**Lord Provost** John Millar	E G Glendinning City of Edinburgh District Council City Chambers High Street Edinburgh EH1 1YJ	031 225 2424
East Lothian District:	**Chairman** Thomas White	D B Millar East Lothian District Council County Buildings Haddington East Lothian EH31 3HA	062 082 416

| Midlothian District: | **Convener**
David R Smith | P W Duguid
Midlothian District Council
1 White Hart Street
Dalkeith
Midlothian
EH22 1DE | 031 663 2880 |

| West Lothian
District: | **Convener**
William Connolly | D A M Morrison
West Lothian District
Council
South Bridge Street
Bathgate
EH48 1TS | Bathgate 53861 |

| **Region**
STRATHCLYDE | **Convener**
Rev Geoffrey Shaw | **Chief Executive**
Dr Lawrence Boyle
Strathclyde Regional Council
Melrose House
19 Cadogan Street
Glasgow   G2 6HR | **Telephone**
041 204 2800 |

| Argyle and Bute
District: | **Chairman**
E T F Spence | M A J Gossip
Argyll and Bute
District Council
Kilmory
Lochgilphead
Argyll
PA31 8RT | Lochgilphead
2177 |

| Bearsden and
Milngavie District: | **Provost**
William Hamilton | A R Rae
Bearsden and Milngavie
District Council
Bodair
Bearsden
Glasgow G61 2TQ | 041 942 2262 |

| City of Glasgow
District: | **Lord Provost**
Peter T McCann | C Murdoch
City of Glasgow
District Council
City Chambers
George Square
Glasgow   G2 1DU | 041 221 9600 |

| Clydebank District: | **Provost**
R Calder | R A Nixon
Clydebank District Council
Muncipal Buildings
Clydebank
G31 1XQ | 041 952 1103 |

| Cumbernauld and
Kilsyth District: | **Chairman**
Gordon Murray | R Kyle MBE
Cumbernauld and
District Council
County Offices
Bron Way
Cumbernauld
Dunbartonshire G67 1 DZ | 02367 22131 |

Cumnock and Doon Valley District:	**Convener** Thomas T McIntyre	D Hemmings Cumnock and Doon Valley District Council Council Offices Lugar Ayrshire KA18 3JQ	0292 669
Cunninghame District:	**Chairman** Dr David White	J M Miller 201 Bridgegate House Bridgegate Irvine KA12 8BD	0294 7416
Dumbarton District:	**Provost** James McKinley	L MacKinnon Dumbarton District Council Crosslet House Dumbarton G82 1QE	0389 6761
East Kilbride District:	**Provost** Mrs Sheila Fin- layson	W G McNay East Kilbride District Council Civic Centre East Kilbride Lanarkshire G74 1AB	03552 2877
Eastwood District:	**Provost** Ian S Hutchison	M D Henry Eastwood District Council Council Offices Cotton Street Paisley PA1 1NE	041 889 545
Hamilton District:	**Chairman** Robert Sherry	W Johnstone Town House 102 Cadzow Street Hamilton Lanarkshire ML3 6HH	06982 2118
Inverclyde District:	**Provost** John Walsh	I C Wilson Inverclyde District Council Muncipal Buildings Greenock Renfrewshire PA15 1LY	0475 2440
Kilmarnock and Loudoun District:	**Chairman** William Aitken	J C W Nicol Kilmarnock and Loudoun District Council Civic Centre Kilmarnock KA1 1BY	0563 21140

Kyle and Carrick District:	**Provost** Alexander D Payton	J R Hill Kyle and Carrick District Council Burns House Statute Square Ayr	0292 81511
Lanark District:	**Convener** Col R C M Monteith MC TD DL	R G Dalkin Lanark District Council 57 High Street Lanark ML11 7LS	0555 61311
Monklands District:	**Provost** Thomas Clarke	James S Ness FCA Monklands District Council Muncipal Buildings Coatbridge Lanarkshire ML5 3LF	0236 24941
Motherwell District:	**Chairman** Hutchison Sneddon OBE	F C Marks Motherwell District Council PO Box 14 Civic Centre Motherwell Lanarkshire ML1 1TW	0698 66166
Renfrew District:	**Provost** Edward Conway	W McIntosh Renfrew District Council Muncipal Buildings Cotton Street Pailsey Renfrewshire PA1 1BU	041 889 5400
Strathkelvin District:	**Chairman** Ian MacBryde	A Harrower Strathkelvin District Council Council Chambers Kirkintilloch Glasgow G66 1PW	041 776 7171

Region TAYSIDE	**Convener** A Millar MC	**Chief Executive** A H Martin Tayside Regional Council PO Box 78 5 Whitehall Crescent Dundee DD1 4AR	**Telephone** 0382 23412 and 22104
Angus District:	**Chairman** Leslie Gray-Cheape	W S McCulloch Angus District Council County Buildings Forfar Angus DD8 3LG	0307 3661

| City of Dundee District: | **Lord Provost** Charles Farquhar | Gordon S Watson City of Dundee District Council City Chambers Dundee DD1 3BY | 0382 23141 |
| Perth and Kinross District: | **Chairman** Thomas McBain | R T Blair Perth and Kinross District Council 3 High Street Perth PB1 1BU | 0738 21222 |

Islands Area Councils

ORKNEY	George R Marnick	H A Graeme Lapsley Orkney Islands Area Council County Offices Kirkwall Orkney KW15 1NY	0856 2310
SHETLAND	Alexander Tulloch	I R Clark Shetland Islands Area Council Town Hall Lerwick Shetland ZE1 0HD	Lerwick 2009
WESTERN ISLES	Rev Donald Macauley	R MacIver Western Isles Area Council County Offices Stornoway Isle of Lewis PA87 2BW	Stornoway 3440

154